Realizing Community Futures

Realizing Community Futures

A Practical Guide to Harnessing Natural Resources

Jerry Vanclay, Ravi Prabhu and Fergus Sinclair

London • Sterling, VA

First published by Earthscan in the UK and USA in 2006

ISBN-10:   1-84407-383-1   paperback
                1-84407-384-X   hardback
ISBN-13:   978-1-84407-383-2   paperback
                978-1-84407-384-9   hardback

Typeset by Safehouse Creative
Printed and bound in the UK by TJ International, Padstow, Cornwall
Cover design by Susanne Harris

For a full list of publications please contact:

Earthscan
8–12 Camden High Street
London, NW1 0JH, UK
Tel: +44 (0)20 7387 8558
Fax: +44 (0)20 7387 8998
Email: earthinfo@earthscan.co.uk
Web: **www.earthscan.co.uk**

22883 Quicksilver Drive, Sterling, VA 20166-2012, USA

Earthscan is an imprint of James and James (Science Publishers) Ltd and publishes in association
with the International Institute for Environment and Development

A catalogue record for this book is available from the British Library

Library of Congress Cataloging-in-Publication Data
Vanclay, Jerome K.
  Realizing community futures : a practical guide to harnessing natural resources / Jerry Vanclay,
Ravi Prabhu, and Fergus Sinclair.
      p. cm.
  Includes bibliographical references.
  ISBN-13: 978-1-84407-384-9 (alk. paper)
  ISBN-10: 1-84407-384-X (alk. paper)
  ISBN-13: 978-1-84407-383-2 (pbk. : alk. paper)
  ISBN-10: 1-84407-383-1 (pbk. : alk. paper)
  1. Natural resources–Management–Citizen participation–Mathematical models. 2. Group deci-
sion-making–Mathematical models. I. Prabhu, Ravi. II. Sinclair, Fergus L. III. Title.
  HC85.V36 2007
  333.701'5195–dc22
                          2006016204

Contents

List of Boxes, Figures and Tables   ix

Foreword   xi

Preface   xiii

Acknowledgements   xv

1   Bringing shared visions to life   1

2   Diverse interests and common problems   9

3   Shared visions   31

4   Explicit visions   63

5   Substantive visions   87

6   Exploring alternatives   111

7   Into the future   133

Resources   *143*

Boxes, Figures and Tables

Boxes

2.1 One thing leads to another in Palawan 17

2.2 A tale of two islands 19

3.1 Current and future scenarios 39

4.1 Helping people to participate 66

Figures

1.1 Batanai broomgrass workers with handcrafted bindings 3

2.1 Rajendra Singh describing a johad 11

3.1 Mangu Lal Patel 34

3.2 Women commencing construction of a new johad 36

3.3 Richard urging broomgrass collectors to develop a vision 37

3.4 Influences identified at an early stage of the ZimFlores model 53

3.5 A lever makes things happen, sometimes in remote times and places (railway on Dartmoor) 56

4.1 A simple grey model of groundwater extraction 70

4.2 A simple model of water extraction with daily consumption of 30 kilolitres per day, and its simulation output as a graph showing groundwater levels over 500 days 71

4.3 Grey model of the first village johad 72

4.4 Grey model of the first village johad with submodel structure 74

4.5 Grey submodel of multiple johads extracted from the model in Figure 4.4 75

4.6 Grey model of river flow with variable numbers of johads 76

4.7 Whiteboard model developed by the broomgrass collectors 82

4.8 Simile model constructed by the broomgrass collectors 82

4.9 The BroomGrass model after tidying up by an experienced modeller 83

5.1 The run button on the Simile toolbar 89

5.2 A small johad at Gopalpura, Rajasthan 90

5.3	Slider to allow size of johads to be varied during simulations	91
5.4	Simile representation of the RiverMaker, showing detail only for the surface water submodel	94
5.5	Detail of johad submodel showing the use of intermediate variables	95
5.6	Diagram showing johad represented as an inverted pyramid	96
5.7	The modelling cycle showing where it is important to focus, idealise and simplify	98
5.8	Example of land tenure implemented in Simile	100
6.1	Simulation of catchments with and without johads, showing the impact on cumulative river flow (gigalitres) and the moderating effect of johads in slowing run-off and maintaining base-flow during the dry season	116
6.2	Simulation run with the BroomGrass model showing grass biomass and household wealth for business as usual and under the new initiatives, simulated for 50 months (4 years)	118
6.3	Gababe broomgrass collectors with their new brooms	119
6.4	Simulation showing the expected impact of extra patrols by forest officers	120
6.5	Simulation of broomgrass reforms, with more equitable sharing of common resources and greater value adding to brooms	121
6.6	Some useful indicators of the effect of johads include the percentage of days with water in wells and depth of water in wells	123

Table

| 3.1 | Selected issues, options and indicators identified by participants at the first modelling workshop | 43 |

Foreword

If you have been in the business of sustainable development over the last few decades, you will be very familiar with a variety of concepts that have been widely used in the rhetoric, in the policies and in the literature. Whether as policy-maker or practitioner, you will have fretted over the challenge of how to put into operation the diversity of lofty philosophy, principles and practices that comprise the overarching concept of sustainable development; and over how to treat simultaneously with the multiple and inter-connected issues that come into play, especially within systems of governance, public organization and administration that are centralized, sectoral and uncoordinated.

Well, help is now at hand; especially for those who seek to advance the concept of sustainable development through the complexity of managing land and landscapes, forests and fields. It comes in the form of this book – a practitioner's 'how to':

- how to reflect a vision into various scenarios;
- how to realize a scenario into reality;
- how to reconcile multiple and often conflicting perspectives;
- how to recognize, evaluate and select among trade-offs.

The approaches and tools that are presented here are not novel – they emerge from observation, analysis, refinement and adaptation by researchers of long-standing attempts to bring the buzzwords into being – participatory management, devolution, subsidiarity, community involvement, adaptive management... The value of this book is that it describes how these approaches and tools have been tried and tested among communities in multiple locations – Zimbabwe, Indonesia, Cameroon – and this experience is now brought together in practical and user-friendly guidelines that can be adapted and applied in many places and scenarios.

Scenarios are ways of visioning futures that we may wish to achieve or to avoid, and the process for exploring them is as important as its products. Scenario exercises thus involve the people, embody the principles and indicate the policies that are relevant to any such future. This book not only encourages us to translate visions of sustainable development into scenarios; it also presents practical guidelines of how to do so, as well as approaches that might inform policies and tools that might aid their implementation.

The principles and practices of sustainable development, it is often said, exist more in rhetoric than in reality. Here is a book that would help us to bridge that gap and to work towards achieving the futures we wish to experience or to bequeath.

Angela Cropper
President, The Cropper Foundation
Port of Spain, July 2006

Preface

What lies still is easy to grasp;
What lies far off is easy to anticipate;
What is brittle is easy to shatter;
What is small is easy to disperse.

Yet a tree broader than a man can embrace is born of a tiny shoot;
A dam greater than a river can overflow starts with a clod of earth;
A journey of a thousand miles begins at the spot under one's feet.

Therefore deal with things before they happen;
Create order before there is confusion.

Lao Tzu, *Tao Te Ching* (Path of the Way)

This book aims to foster enthusiasm for structured learning and participatory modelling in natural resource management by illustrating highlights of our collective experience using these techniques. We have tried to write in a way that helps others to learn *from* our experience, not *about* it. In doing this, we have glossed over some of the blind alleys that we went down, and documented what, with the benefit of hindsight, we would have done, rather than telling the story in the way that it unfolded (for a fuller account, see the website or CD supporting this book – details of how to access these are on page 143. We hope that by relating our experiences in this way, we will encourage others to try these approaches, especially in situations where problems are chronic, or have proved difficult to resolve with more traditional methods.

One of our examples in this book is about the River-maker, Rajendra Singh, who was motivated to effective action by Mangu Lal Patel, the wise old man from the village of Gopalpura. Mangu advised '*Thein to kuch karo Rajendra, kal favte gonti ler agyo*' (Go and do something Rajendra, bring spade tomorrow and start work). So too, we urge you not just to read about these approaches to structured learning and participatory modelling, but to go and try them, tomorrow!

Acknowledgements

Much of our journey in developing the ideas for this book was undertaken in the company of Mandy Haggith. She provided a great deal of the inspiration to write a book of this nature. Mandy would certainly have written it differently, but we would like to acknowledge her contribution to many of the approaches that we have set out here. Robert Muetzelfeldt pioneered the concept of visual modelling environments accessible to everyone involved in natural resource management and Jasper Taylor helped him to realize this as Simile. They were fellow travellers on the journey to develop the FLORES approach to landscape-scale modelling; without them, much of what is described in the latter half of this book would remain an empty shell.

Richard Nyirenda, Tendayi Mutimukuru, Wavell Standa-Gunda, Liswe Sibanda and the 'broomgrass ladies' from Mafungautsi were all the inspiration we needed to realise that it was time to take participatory modelling and scenario development out of the domain of 'experts' and into everyday life. Their work is a crucial part of this book. Herry Purnomo tested some of the ideas that we set out here and, together with Edwin Yulianto and Theo Zacharias, helped turn them into working tools. Rajendra Singh-ji warmly welcomed us in India and graciously agreed to let us use his work and life as an example to inspire the use of the techniques that we set out in the book.

Much of the work underpinning this book was supported by the UK Department for International Development (DFID), FRP projects R7315 and R7635, but the views expressed are not necessarily those of DFID. John Palmer paved the way for our first tentative steps, by helping to fund the Bukittinggi workshop, and the participants of that workshop gave us great confidence and encouragement. Many other people have helped us along the way.

As authors, we are pleased to acknowledge the help of so many people in bringing this book into being but, of course, remain solely responsible for the final content. We hope this book is useful, and helps to repay the debt that we owe to so many.

Jerry Vanclay   *Ravi Prabhu*   *Fergus Sinclair*
Lismore   *Harare*   *Bangor*

Introduction: Bringing shared visions to life

I'm kind of homesick for a country
To which I've never been before;
No sad goodbyes will there be spoken,
And time won't matter any more.

I'm looking now across the river
Where my faith will end in sight …

Squire E. Parsons Jr, *Beulah Land*[1]

Mrs Siwela is all smiles. Her brooms, with their elegant handcrafted binding, have won a prize at the Gweru Agricultural Show and are selling well, lifting her and her family out of debt. She is reaping the rewards of a new way to solve problems in which she and her neighbours formulated a plan that helped them to improve their own livelihoods. Not only is she better off, but she has new-found confidence and an enthusiasm to control her own destiny. She achieved this through a process in which she and her neighbours shared their vision for the future, constructed a formal model of their understanding of the resources at their disposal, and then used the model to explore a range of options that might help them to reach their vision. There are many situations, the world over, where people and natural resources interact in this way.

Figure 1.1 Batanai broomgrass workers with handcrafted bindings
Source: Ravi Prabhu

This book is about encouraging people to share visions and helping them to progress from these visions to take appropriate actions that will help realize their visions. The choice of appropriate actions is a key aspect of this book and we dwell on some ways to ensure that chosen actions are effective ways to make progress in realizing a vision.

While much of what we introduce here is new, the underpinning concept is as old as civilization itself. Ever since people first began to use tools thousands of years ago, they have sought to depict the world around them, through cave paintings and dance rituals rich in symbolism and allegory. People not only depicted the world as it was, but also as they wanted it to be. In this book, we draw on this innate ability of people to imagine an achievable future and offer techniques to help realize that future.

Depending on our circumstances and frame of mind – who we are, where we live and what resources we can access – the future may look bleak or rosy. Nonetheless, irrespective of our situation, most of us dream of a better future. Often such dreams are not idle daydreams, but are visions of a future that can be attained – if enough people share the vision and are prepared to cooperate. This book is about how to take such a dream and turn it into reality.

A simple example

The people of Batanai village in central Zimbabwe knew that their broomgrass harvest was not sustainable, but until they met Richard, they could not see an alternative – they had to feed and clothe their families so they had to carry on harvesting broomgrass. Richard Nyirenda[2] gained their confidence and introduced the concepts of structured learning and participatory modelling. These processes helped the villagers gain a new understanding of their broomgrass resource and the marketing opportunities for their products. With the help of Richard and his team, the broomgrass workers developed a shared vision, formulated a model that allowed them to explore their options, brainstormed to find innovative options, and devised a way to realize their vision. They gained the confidence to put these ideas into practice and empowered themselves to create and adhere to new communal rules to achieve fair and wise use of their communal resources. As a result, the broomgrass on the *vlei* (a seasonally inundated grassland) is now more productive, people are making better brooms, and they are earning more money than ever before. In Batanai, structured learning through participatory modelling has been the catalyst that has helped the community to change its destiny.

The range of applications

This book draws on three case studies. We have already outlined the case of the broomgrass collectors in Batanai, a simple case study dealing with a single resource (broomgrass), a small community (the broomgrass collectors of Batanai village), a confined location (the *vlei*), and a limited time-frame (a few years). However, the techniques we describe are not confined to such simple situations. On the contrary, the benefits of structured learning become more apparent in more complex situations where these methods of coping with complexity may reveal ways forward that might otherwise not be found.

We offer two such examples. Rajendra Singh, the River-maker, has received many accolades for bringing rivers back to life in arid Rajasthan. In his work, Rajendra encountered considerable opposition from various vested interests. We illustrate how construction and discussion of simulation models could have helped to overcome this opposition and to explore consequences more productively. The River-maker case study is wider in scope than the broomgrass case study because it deals with the availability of surface water and groundwater at the catchment scale, and because it is affected by people's support for, and opposition to, constructing percolation tanks that harvest surface water. Our third case study is even more ambitious and deals with chronic deterioration of several natural resources in the Mafungautsi region of Zimbabwe. It deals with forests, crops, rangelands, water, livestock, and people and their land use decisions, all interacting at the landscape scale and affected by people's decisions about land use. There is no pressing problem that needs to be solved; rather there is an awareness of a chronic situation in which several resources (including social capital) are slowly being depleted without any durable benefit to society. The core of all three case studies is an intimate interaction between people and natural resources.

Each of the simulation models developed has different characteristics. The River-maker case study deals with daily rainfall but looks at catchment-wide impacts on river flow and water depth in wells over several years. The broomgrass case study uses monthly harvests to examine what will happen to the broomgrass on the *vlei* over a few short years, while the Mafungautsi case study deals with many weekly events to make inferences about a wide range of resources at the landscape scale over many years. The structured learning and participatory modelling approaches that we advocate are equally applicable to all these diverse situations. In each case, the models and resulting ideas about what might happen to natural resources if different actions are taken have been made by local people rather than external experts. Certainly, these people were sometimes guided by experienced facilitators, and we do emphasize the need for good technical support, but everything we advocate in this book is designed to be accessible and useful to anyone who wishes to try.

Route map of the book

We have promised to help you – the reader – and your team to take a dream and turn it into reality. This can be and has been done using several steps that form the chapters of this book:

1   recognize the potential (this chapter);
2   agree on a common problem;
3   share a vision;
4   make that vision explicit;
5   substantiate assumptions;
6   explore options and implications;
7   implement what has been learned.

Hopefully, this brief introduction has served to whet your appetite. We now continue to examine how to find common ground among people with diverse interests.

Notes

1   'Beulah Land' (1979) words and music by Squire E. Parsons Jr, available at www.squireparsons.com.
2   T. Mutimukuru, R. Nyirenda and F. Matose (2004) 'Learning amongst ourselves: Adaptive forest management through social learning in Zimbabwe', in C. J. P. Colfer (ed) *The Equitable Forest: Diversity and Community in Sustainable Resource Management*, Resources for the Future, pp186–206.

2

Diverse interests and common problems

My daddy used to tell me don't be fooled by what you see
If you want to get to the heart of things you gotta look way down deep ...
There's a mighty river flowing where the water's cool and sweet
Don't be fooled by a muddy stream, be careful where you drink
Life is what you make it sometimes a living hell
If you want to find that promised land dig a little deeper in the well

Roger Bowling and Jody Emerson,
'Dig a Little Deeper in the Well'[1]

Rajendra Singh has been called the 'River-maker' for his work in bringing dead rivers back to life in India's desert state of Rajasthan. At a time when there is widespread recognition of the scarcity of water, it is not surprising that he has received many awards for his work, including the prestigious Ramon Magsaysay award for community leadership.[2] After all, it seems obvious that quenching thirst in a dry and dusty region is in everyone's interest. Well, it may surprise you to learn that this was not the case, and that Rajendra Singh has faced strong opposition from rural élites and government officials, who for different reasons felt that his work was counter to their interests. On one occasion he suffered a fractured skull after a particularly heated debate with rural government officials! The rural élites – mainly power brokers and money lenders – were concerned that more water in the landscape would lead to economic empowerment of the poor, which

Figure 2.1 Rajendra Singh describing a johad
Source: Fergus Sinclair

could liberate these farmers from their clutches. The government irrigation department felt that the traditional systems of water harvesting advocated by Rajendra Singh challenged their scientific knowledge base and threatened their authority and power. So although everyone in that part of India recognized water scarcity as a serious problem, their interests were very divergent. In a sense Rajendra Singh had it easy because at least there was agreement about the common problem, namely the shortage of water in the dark zone, that part of the country where there was no groundwater.

All natural resources management contexts are characterized by a multitude of interests. Sometimes these interests conflict and compound problems, but in most cases, the key obstacle is that there is no shared understanding of what the problems might be. Here we look at the people, the nature of their problems and the diversity of their interests as the starting point of a journey towards developing common visions and collaborative actions to improve the future.

Setting the stage

People are the key to resolving resource conflicts. There is no doubt that it is important to understand how ecosystems work and how to harness their productivity to meet human needs, both now and in the future, but people are the key to success in moving towards improved management of these resources. To make progress towards improving the benefits derived from managed natural resources, we need to know three things:

1   Who has an interest in these resources?
2   What is the nature of their interest?
3   What do they see as the main constraints to realizing their interest?

Given that we are dealing with complex systems where information deficits and uncertainty are prominent features, we expect that there will always be opportunities for improvement. The challenge is to identify the stake-holders, recognize their interests, and diagnose the system. This leads to three key concepts that set the stage for further discussion about better outcomes: first, stakeholders (those who have an interest in the resources); second, their diverse interests in and perceptions of the problem (and of potential solutions); and third, the complex natural and social interactions involved in natural resource systems.

Stakeholders

Natural resources such as water, forests or fisheries involve many different kinds of people who use, control or have some other interest in these re-sources. Exactly who these people are and what they do depend on the na-ture of the resource, its geographic extent and the time-scale over which the resource is used. Our River-maker case study with Rajendra Singh involved micro-catchments with small areas (usually less than 1000 hectares) and short time frames (5–10 years). Key stakeholder groups included local vil-lagers, Rajendra's local team (Tarun Bhagat Sangh or TBS, the Young India Association), district officials, water engineers, local businessmen and local politicians. Clearly, with many issues, stakeholders can be diverse and dis-persed individuals and associations. In Rajendra's case, the key stakeholders changed considerably over time as Rajendra's influence and fame spread.

Other situations may involve very different stakeholder groups. The diversity of stakeholders in our Mafungautsi case study re-flects recent land-use trends. The Mafungautsi forest reserve is surrounded by lands that were traditionally farmed for subsistence needs but were ex-periencing a rapid expansion of commercial cotton cropping. The forest itself protects part of the catchment of Lake Kariba, a major irrigation and hydroelectric facility. Thus stakeholders include forestry officials, ru-ral development agencies, the irrigation department, agricultural extension agents, local farmers, village leaders and other representatives of the local community, local users involved in harvesting and processing forest produce, politicians, police, traders and transporters of products from the forest, to name just a few.

This rich diversity of stakeholders is not confined to our case studies but reflects reality. Even in the simplest cases (for example, a single resource confined to a solitary village), we find that stakeholders are not homogenous: they are differentiated by class, caste and ethnicity, by gender and wealth, and by physical access to forests and community centres. These attributes translate into differences in interests, needs and capacities, as well as differentiated access to decision making, to forest resources and to opportunities for livelihood enhancement. It is often the case that marginalized groups and individuals have the least access to common property resources such as forests. Nonetheless, forests are often critical in sustaining these marginalized members of communities, both for their subsistence and for income generation needs.

In the process of moving forward from dreams and desires to concrete actions it is important to recognize stakeholders and identify the nature of their interest in the resource (or in the 'dream'). CIFOR[3] researcher Carol Colfer has developed a simple method to determine 'who counts' in forest management.[4] The method involves a simple scoring system based on characteristics such as proximity, power and dependence on the forest. Other experience suggests an additional consideration: never omit anyone who may subsequently derail the process.

Another important consideration is the nature of the relationships between the various stakeholders. These relations are seldom straightforward as they may be burdened by memories of past conflicts and other experiences. Conflicts often arise around access rights to resources, organizational issues, representation on relevant decision-making bodies, distribution and sale of products, fund mobilization and delineation of boundaries.

It is vital to be aware that stakeholders are a dynamic group with changing membership, different needs and interests, and a history of relationships with each other.

Diverse interests

We saw in the case of Rajendra Singh how a relatively straightforward problem of providing water could generate very different interests. This is not
an isolated case. Most situations will have as many interests represented as
there are groups of stakeholders. For instance, in the Mafungautsi State
Forest, the Forestry Commission's interest is to protect the forest from illegal harvesting of timber and other products such as honey, thatchgrass
and broomgrass, while at the same time generating sufficient benefits for
neighbouring communities to keep them from invading the forest. The
communities have diverse interests of their own. Some of them had previously been expelled from the forest and want their ancestral land back,
while others are interested in being able to earn some cash income from the
forest to augment the subsistence farming they undertake. A more ambitious group would like to have access to some of the valuable timber left in
the forest, but the Zimbabwe Forestry Commission does not permit this as
it believes this would be detrimental to the forest. Still others are interested
in using the committees set up by the Forestry Commission to manage the
harvesting of non-timber forest products to consolidate their influence in
their villages. The different ethnic groups in the area have different cultural
affiliations to the forest, dictating different interests. Women tend to have
a greater interest in the grasses, for thatching or broom production, while
the men prefer to focus on honey collection and timber. Children may be
required to herd livestock and collect fruit. All this occurs at the so-called
'community level'. This diversity within the community mirrors the het-
erogeneity of ethnicity, gender, age groups, livelihood strategies, political
ambitions, education levels and so on. To add further confusion, people
may be wary of revealing their interests for fear that this may have nega-
tive repercussions of one kind or another, and they themselves may not be
entirely clear about their interests.

      Further up the political hierarchy, the diversity of inter-
ests at the district, province or state level remains equally high, but actors at

this level tend to be individuals representing organizations and institutions, rather than individuals representing households. Although education levels may be generally higher, the positions tend to be more entrenched and the agendas that underlie professed interests often tend to be more obscure.

Interests are dynamic; they change in response to developments in the external world and in response to psychological and social changes within the individuals and groups concerned as a result of their own development. Finding out about people's real interests is often a slow process that involves building trust, finding ways to communicate that are acceptable to everyone concerned, and demonstrating the ability to listen and understand. All this takes time. But a failure to understand interests properly can easily lead to failure in any project or undertaking that touches on those interests.

One of the best ways to determine people's interests is to provide them with the space and the opportunity to articulate their interests *to each other* in a facilitated process of visioning and scenario exploration. We deal with this process in more detail from Chapter 3 onwards.

Complexity

A web is frequently used as a metaphor to describe complexity, as it signifies multiple interconnections in a pattern that is intricate, but describable. People speak of the 'web of life' and mean the multiple interconnections between the various strands of life. But a web is an inadequate metaphor because it is usually imagined as a flat and unchanging structure. In contrast, complex systems are multi-dimensional and change all the time. Because they are linked, one part of a complex system can affect another part of the system. And because they are linked in many different ways, it is not always clear what the nature of the effect may be, when it may become evident, or indeed how many different effects there are. Moreover the interconnections mean that the influence can go both ways; there can be feedback from the component being affected back to the initiating component. Consider also that events in the distant past can affect the present. It is no wonder that uncertainty and surprise are close companions of complex systems. Managing natural resources at almost any scale is essentially an exercise in trying to harness a complex human-ecological system for a restricted but changing set of goals.

Box 2.1 relates how two colleagues of ours, Herlina Hartanto and Cris Lorenzo,[5] working on the island of Palawan in the Philippines, discovered that changes to one part of a complex system quite unexpectedly changed another part of the system.

Box 2.1 One thing leads to another in Palawan

Recently, the villages of San Rafael, Tanabag and Concepcion on the island of Palawan got together and applied for permission to manage about 5000 hectares as a community forest. As part of their efforts to improve management they began to collaborate in monitoring the forest. Their monitoring included a record of the volumes of almaciga resin extracted. Somewhat to their surprise they learnt that they were not collecting as much resin as they had expected. They suspected that this was due to the illegal extraction activities taking place in the area. They subsequently expanded their monitoring to assess and control these illegal activities in coordination with concerned government agencies, and with community groups such as the Bataks, Tagbanuas and local fishermen. This collaboration helped to settle a long-standing dispute with the Batak community over the use of non-timber forest products, and led to an ongoing agreement to exchange information on management, harvesting and processing techniques.

Coming to grips with the complexity that is inherent in a natural resources management situation requires an understanding of the links in the system – the people in their various social and economic organizations and networks, the ecology of the resource, the policy and political environment, markets and so on. Understanding the structure (namely, the way these components are linked to each other) and the overall behaviour (the 'emergent' properties) are the two important steps involved in gaining this understanding. The rest of this book is about how to attain these insights.

It is not possible to tame complexity entirely because uncertainty defies any kind of management. But it is possible to try and understand the nature of the dynamic complexity and to set up management systems so that they are resilient to the shocks and surprises that result from uncertainty.

Dealing with uncertainty: Building resilience

'Survival of the fittest' is a metaphor that more or less reflects Charles Darwin's views[6] on evolution and the emergence of new species. It evokes images of a struggle between species for resources in a battle to survive. Competition is the dominant social force in the metaphor. The same metaphor is used to justify the dynamics of the economic market-place and we are told that this is in our interest as only the fittest companies and the best products will survive. Like any metaphor, this is only partially true and because there is another side to this coin, buying into it too fully can be dangerous. So what is the other side of the coin? We describe it with another metaphor from the eminent scientist Lynn Margulis[7] who has countered that life did not take over the planet by combat but by cooperation, partnership and networking. Collaboration is evident in all communities ranging from bacteria and lichen to complex ecosystems and social organizations. Shashi Kant, an economist who was recently recognized with a prestigious award,[8] has called for a reappraisal of economic theory to account for altruistic

Box 2.2 A tale of two islands

Easter Island lies in the Pacific Ocean, just south of the Tropic of Capricorn and 4000 kilometres from South America. When first settled about AD 400, it was richly vegetated, but at the time of first European contact in 1722, the island was desolate. During that time, a great civilization developed and collapsed. Jared Diamond[9] has written about the rise and fall of civilization on Easter Island (and in other places), the failure to anticipate the extent of deforestation, the consequences for their ability to catch fish, and the subsequent decline into civil war and cannibalism.

St Helena is geographically somewhat similar to Easter Island, lying in the Atlantic Ocean, 2000 kilometres from the coast of Africa. When first settled in the early 1500s St Helena was richly vegetated, but by 1700 the vegetation was in serious decline. However, unlike the Easter Islanders, the people of St Helena recognized the problem, anticipated its severity, and called a public meeting to discuss possible courses of action. A law was proposed to the governor commanding the destruction of all the goats and sheep for a period of ten years from February 1731. This was successful, and 'indigenous trees shot up spontaneously in great numbers'.[10] Feral goats continued to be a problem until the 1960s, but sufficient native vegetation remained to warrant the creation of Diana's Peak National Park in 1996, a tribute to the foresight and action of ordinary people back in 1731.

behaviour, recognizing that people can benefit themselves by helping others. Clearly, collaboration is important in ecology, economics and society.

The other great social force needed to deal with complexity and uncertainty is the ability to learn. All sentient living things have an ability to learn from experience. Human beings also have the ability to reason based on this experience and to project it into the future as a basis for decision making. While evolution may be the basis for survival of a species, learning is the basis for individual and societal adaptation and therefore survival of civilizations, cultures and social groups (see Box 2.2). Fostering collaboration and learning is the key to developing the capacity to adapt quickly and successfully. It is this capacity to adapt that affords living organisms and societies alike the resilience to deal with the uncertainty that our wonderfully dynamic and complex world generates. In this section we briefly explore collaboration and learning as the strategies that underpin our ability to realize our visions.

Shared understanding

It can be difficult to create a shared understanding of a problem among diverse stakeholders. Success must involve collaboration, communication and mutual learning, and may require facilitation. However, a shared understanding of a common problem provides the foundation necessary for visioning, finding and implementing durable solutions, so we spend some time examining how to develop a shared understanding of problems and interests.

We have seen that there are diverse interests involved in most natural resources. In the same way, we can see that knowledge about how to manage and use these resources and to build and maintain the framework for management is fragmented. Different parts of the local community have different pieces of this knowledge, and much of it is held outside the local community by extension agents, scientists and other so-called experts. Knowledge held by this latter group is often not accessible because the people who need it most are those least able to access it. This may be because those who need it do not know that this knowledge exists, or how to access it, or it may be because the information is in a form that is not useful, because it is in a scientific article full of technical jargon, or in a language that is not spoken locally. Clearly it is important to find ways of synthesizing and supplementing knowledge that already exists. More importantly, however, information should be made more readily available to those who need it most. Sharing information requires two-way communication, and needs action for learning to take place.

When our colleague Richard Nyirenda set out to try to facilitate the development of a management system built on collaboration and learning in the Mafungautsi area of Zimbabwe, he faced a whole series of problems. The people in the area had long been used to the government making all the decisions about the forest, they felt they had little power and had fallen into a passive role with respect to taking management initiatives. The Shangwe, who were the original inhabitants of the area and were the more intensive forest users, did not want to cooperate and share their knowledge with the more recently arrived Shona farmers. The women in the area were the ones who traditionally harvested broomgrass and thatchgrass, the two major products that local people were officially allowed to harvest. Yet women were under-represented at all gatherings where decisions about the resource were made. Even when they were present, Richard noted that they remained silent and in the background. Clearly here was a situation in which there were several different interests, and where knowledge about forest resources was dispersed, and where power was distributed across several groups and individuals, including the government Forestry Commission. Yet the barriers to communicating and developing a shared understanding were high. Passiveness, distrust and differences in power, education and gender were just some of the constraints. Others included poverty, physical distance from meeting places and competing demands on time of the local stakeholders. Richard wanted to use visioning and experiential learning techniques to help catalyse mutually beneficial management, but he realized this would have to wait until at least some of the barriers to communication and understanding had been removed.

This is not an unusual situation. As we have seen in the case of Rajendra Singh, although a solution may be glaringly obvious, achieving it in a manner that ensures the support of all stakeholders can be tricky. Careful thought needs to be given to the barriers to communication, collaboration and learning that exist in any community or group. Only when these have been recognized is it possible to begin to devise a plan to deal with them. In any case this plan must be devised together with a majority, if not all, of the important stakeholders involved, if it is to have any meaning beyond the paper on which it has been conceived.

In Richard's case, he decided to try to deal with two key constraints, the general passiveness of local stakeholders and the reluctance of the women to engage in any public discussions on managing the forest resources. To counter the passiveness he organized a number of workshops on 'training for transformation', a technique developed by Anne Hope and Sally Timmel,[11] during their work in Zimbabwe in the 1980s, when they wrestled with overcoming the root causes of fatalism and apathy among rural communities in newly independent Zimbabwe. This technique was based on the teachings of Paulo Freire,[12] who stipulated that transformation has to come from within and that education should encourage action and reflection. The second thing Richard did was a great deal simpler – his facilitation team was expanded to include a woman researcher, Tendayi Mutimukuru.[13] Within days of both these actions having been taken, it was clear that sufficient space and momentum had been created for the local stakeholders to start engaging with each other in intensive sessions of visioning and planning. The dam had quite perceptibly been broken, and the process of joining up knowledge and generating a shared understanding could now begin.

To the north of Mafungautsi in a peri-urban community near Zomba in Malawi, another researcher, James Milner[14] was facing similar problems. Here the issue was how best to join hands to manage eucalyptus plantations established by a development project on Ntonya Hill. These plantations were shared across the land of several villages dotted around the hill. Try as he might, James was unable to create suitable conditions to foster a shared understanding of how to move forward. Like Rajendra Singh, he was faced with a powerful adversary, this time a traditional chief who felt that James's efforts to bring people together around the subject of the plantations undermined his authority and therefore his source of income. He simply forbade collaboration with James, and when this did not work, prohibited James's entry into the area. Research in the area on improving management ceased as a result. James's colleagues are trying to engage the chief in a dialogue that is less threatening. This is proving to be a frustratingly slow process! The experience highlights the need to find processes that are non-threatening, that recognize self-interest and that are transparently win–win for all participants. In the Zomba case, the chief needed to be offered a role, and to be reassured that he would gain respect by improving the well-being of his community.

Communities of practice

As individuals begin to share information about a common set of tasks and problems, they begin to build relationships with each other that go beyond the immediate present. They start developing a collective identity around a set of common values. As this begins to happen these individuals begin to form what is being called a 'community of practice': a self-organizing and self-generating network of communications, with a shared purpose and meaning, and a shared culture that results in coordination of behaviour and creation of shared knowledge. In our work we have seen many such communities emerge, in which all members know that they will be supported in their endeavours to achieve their own goals, such as with respect to the harvesting of broomgrass in a forest, carrying out research on poverty alleviation, or in the building of complex system dynamics models.

Etienne Wenger[15] has written much about communities of practice, and characterizes them by three features: mutual engagement of its members, a joint enterprise, and in time, a shared repertoire of routines, tacit rules of conduct and knowledge. In our work in community forests around the world we have begun to recognize such communities of practice as being the basic social building blocks for all meaningful long-term efforts to improve management. In such communities of practice we see the linking of social and communication networks in a manner that transcends the often artificial boundaries of formal organizations. The vitality of any formal organization lies in its communities of practice. This observation applies to many organizations, including large corporations.

Looking for and working with existing communities of practice is important for the success of any endeavour that has a life of more than a few days and involves more than a few people. Most natural resources management endeavours fall in this category.

Effective facilitation

We have talked about the importance of generating shared understandings, of the emergence of communities of practice, and of the need to work with and through them. We have also stressed the importance of these processes in contributing to our initial objective of strengthening collaboration and learning among the stakeholders in a resource. The process of setting these wheels in motion, the role that Rajendra Singh, Richard Nyirenda and James Milner sought to embody, is that of facilitation. Facilitation is different from teaching or mentoring. It is not a one-way activity in which one person is the transmitter and the others receive wisdom. Being an effective facilitator means that you are a co-learner.

Facilitation is often taken to mean the things done by the person who leads a discussion in a workshop; things such as exploring the participants' expectations, ensuring that the discussion is oriented towards meeting the objectives, making sure everyone gets to participate, and so on. While all this and more is indeed part of a facilitator's role, facilitation is much more than making certain that a workshop or a gathering runs smoothly. Facilitation is about guiding a whole process of decision making and action learning to create opportunities for pooling knowledge, skills and abilities within the groups concerned, and accessing information and resources from outside the groups. These opportunities always appear; the challenge for the facilitator is to anticipate them and to seize the moment when it occurs.

For instance, Richard Nyirenda will listen patiently and with great interest, providing visual and social prompts to his partners in dialogue to continue to speak and to share their ideas. Equally he will throw in ideas for people to consider, if he thinks that this might provoke an exploration of new avenues. This is how he introduced the idea of carrying out training for transformation. All our colleagues involved in the research on adaptive collaborative management[16] threw in ideas about learning together and about monitoring, as a group, the progress of plans, or the use of visioning to start things off. So facilitation can be both proactive and reactive. This is not the place to discuss facilitation at length. For those interested in reading more about this fascinating subject we have included a few important references in the Resources section near the end of this book.

In our own work we have used facilitation mainly to enhance shared learning by groups. This kind of learning usually comes from a process of self-development through experience. We know that adults learn best when they are actively involved, if the context of learning can be applied directly to their tasks or jobs, and when they are in control of the learning process. Richard Nyirenda experienced these implications at first hand when his groups redesigned their resource allocation schemes. Previously people had simply gone into the *vlei* to harvest their entitlement of thatchgrass on a first-come, first-served basis. Reflecting on this as more and more people turned to the common land for income in the face of economic adversity, the villagers realized that the system of harvesting was not serving them well. After much discussion and negotiation they designed a system using a simple map of the area, wherein each family was allocated a plot to harvest, and were only allowed to move on to a new area after they had completed their section. This meant that the many widows and orphans who were slower to harvest the thatchgrass could now do so without fear that they would lose their access to the resource.

We are also interested in facilitation because it can be used to improve the connections between people and groups. Recent research suggests that one of the conditions that is conducive to the emergence of novelty is 'better connecting a system to itself'. This means making sure that different parts of a system – for example, a water harvesting group, the rest of the village, the bio-physical resources and the relevant parts of the outside world – are in touch with each other, so that there are sufficient opportunities for feedbacks to take place and be noticed. If the money lenders were really in touch with the needs of the local people in Rajendra Singh's case, they would have realized that more water would have meant more income but also a greater demand for credit. By adjusting their credit policies they may have been able to successfully compete against distant banks or micro-credit schemes and stay in business more effectively.

In our view a facilitator has to be able to hold a vision, to articulate it clearly and to communicate it with passion and charisma. They must be a person whose actions embody certain values that serve as a standard for others to strive for. One of their aims would be to facilitate the emergence of novelty. This means creating conditions, rather than giving directions, and using the power of authority to empower others.

Collaboration, learning and implications for management

Having outlined the importance of collaboration and learning as cornerstones for good management in the previous sections, let us take a look at what this means in terms of a management system. All management systems call for some measure of collaboration and learning, no matter how efficient they are. Even in a very hierarchical organization, the leadership is dependent on the cooperation of all staff if the organization is to function efficiently. Such organizations also learn, although the learning is concentrated mainly at the level of the top decision makers, simply because they have staked out for themselves the right to make the decisions that entail change. Most government bureaucracies operate in this fashion, some of them quite successfully.

When we advocate the importance of collaboration and of learning we are not suggesting anything new. Or are we? Our emphasis lies on management systems that actively seek to exploit opportunities for collaboration and learning in a planned and structured manner. There are quite a few models of such management approaches and they have been given a variety of names from 'adaptive management systems' through to 'learning organizations'. In their approach and in their thrust these models are the same. The differences may lie in the domain (for example, private industry) that they are applied to, or the sector (adaptive management systems have been applied mainly to fisheries and to a lesser extent to forests) or to the scale of application. Most of these approaches have stressed learning more than they have collaboration.

We have been involved in a four-year research programme that has sought to understand the impacts of emphasizing both learning and collaboration. The approach tested under this programme involving forest areas in ten countries across Asia, Africa and Latin America goes appropriately by the name of adaptive collaborative management[17] (ACM). Essentially ACM can be described as a series of steps on a spiral of learning and improvement, or a loop that begins with understanding who should be involved and ends with adjustments of plans and actions. ACM seeks to strengthen and enhance processes of adaptation so that the groups concerned have the capacity to adapt more quickly and more appropriately than by simple trial and error to the processes of rapid change that confront them.

The essence of an adaptive collaborative approach to natural resources management is that stakeholders use intentional ongoing learning as the fundamental basis for decision making and planning in community forest management, and work towards effective communication among stakeholders, including input to decision making, conflict management and collective actions. Intentional learning[18] not only includes the building or transfer of knowledge and skills, but also social and transformative learning processes where people or groups of people share experiences, perspectives and knowledge for both communication and critical reflection, as a means of jointly understanding and addressing (that is, creating change regarding) shared challenges. As a part of this, an adaptive approach to management encourages forest managers from the local to the national level to practise visioning, monitoring and ongoing critical reflection and negotiation. An ACM approach also encourages stakeholders to consider the dynamic and interconnected nature of human and natural systems in their planning processes and to continually build capacities for dealing with critical uncertainties and risks.

Having established a meaningful social context, we can now get on with the details of how to use visioning and scenario exploration based on computer simulations.

Notes

1   'Dig a little deeper in the well' (1979) Words and
        music by Roger Bowling and Jody Emerson, sung by
        The Oak Ridge Boys.

2   Ramon Del Fierro Magsaysay (1907–1957) was
        President of the Republic of the Philippines from
        1953 to 1957. The Ramon Magsaysay award
        recognizes his efforts to foster freedom, equality and
        happiness for all, and is awarded annually to honour
        'greatness of spirit shown in service to the people.'
        Rajendra's 2001 award recognizes 'leadership of a
        community toward helping the disadvantaged have
        fuller opportunities and a better life.' See www.rmaf.
        org.ph.

3   CIFOR is the Center for International Forest
        Research, an institute researching 'Science for Forests
        and People'. See www.cifor.cgiar.org.

4   C. J. P. Colfer (1995) 'Who counts most in
        sustainable forest management?' Center for

International Forest Research, Working Paper No 7.

5   H. Hartanto, M. C. Lorenzo, C. Valmores, L. Arda-
     Minas, E. M. Burton and R. Prabhu (2003) *Learning
     Together: Responding to Change and Complexity
     to Improve Community Forests in the Philippines*,
     EarthPrint.

6   C. Darwin (1859) *The Origin of Species*, John Murray,
     London.

7   L. Margulis (1998) *Symbiotic Planet: A New Look
     at Evolution*, Basic Books. Also L. Margulis and D.
     Sagan, 2000, *What is Life?* University of California
     Press.

8   Shashi Kant was awarded the 2005 Scientific
     Achievement Award from the International Union
     of Forest Research Organizations. An overview of his
     research is given in S. Kant and R. A. Berry (2005)
     Institutions, Sustainability, and Natural Resources,
     Springer.

9   J. Diamond (1995) 'Easter Island's end', *Discover
     Magazine,* August 1995. Also J. Diamond (2005)
     Collapse: How Societies Choose to Fail or Succeed,
     Viking.

10   T. H. Brooke (1808) *A History of the Island of St
     Helena from its Discovery by the Portuguese to the Year
     1806,* Black, Parry & Kingsbury, London.

11   A. Hope and S. Timmel (1995) *Training for
     Transformation*, three volume set, Intermediate
     Technology Development Group Publishing.
     Also A. Hope and S. Timmel (1999) *Training for
     Transformation, Book 4: A Handbook for Community
     Workers,* ITDG Publishing.

12   Paulo Freire (1921–1997) was a Brazilian educationist
     who was influential in encouraging experiential
     learning and fostering a 'pedagogy of hope'. See www.
     infed.org/thinkers/et-freir.htm.

13   T. Mutimukuru, W. Kozanayi and R. Nyirenda
     (2006) 'Catalyzing collaborative monitoring
     processes in joint forest management situations: The
     Mafungautsi forest case, Zimbabwe', *Society and
     Natural Resources*, vol 19, pp209–224.

14   J. Kamoto and J. Milner (2003) 'Negotiating
     multiple and overlapping claims on land rights:
     Experiences from Malawi', Hawaii International
     Conference on Social Sciences, www.hicsocial.org/
     Social2003Proceedings/Judith%20Kamoto.pdf.

15   E. Wenger (1998) *Communities of Practice*, Cambridge
     University Press, www.ewenger.com/theory/index.
     htm.

16   Adaptive collaborative management is research that
     seeks to understand whether improving collaboration
     and learning in groups will help local communities to
     strengthen their management and adapt successfully
     to changing circumstances.

17   C. J. P. Colfer (2005) *The Complex Forest:
     Communities, Uncertainty, and Adaptive Collaborative
     Management*, Resources for the Future.

18   M. Martinez (1999) 'An investigation into how
     successful learners learn: Measuring the impact of
     learning orientation, a learner-difference variable, on
     learning', Dissertation, Brigham Young University,
     University Microfilms No. 992217.

Shared visions

Let us not wallow in the valley of despair. I say to you today, my friends, that in spite of the difficulties and frustrations of the moment, I still have a dream ...

I have a dream that one day this nation will rise up and live out the true meaning of its creed: 'We hold these truths to be self-evident: that all men are created equal'.

I have a dream that one day on the red hills of Georgia the sons of former slaves and the sons of former slaveowners will be able to sit down together at a table of brotherhood.

I have a dream ...

Dr Martin Luther King[1]

When Martin Luther King inspired a quarter of a million people, saying 'I have a dream …', he unleashed a response that reverberated around the world. It still does. Dreams are powerful motivators that have carried oppressed people to freedom, human beings to the moon, and may yet carry our planet to a sustainable future. They can also simply end up as enjoyable flights of fantasy, daydreams that provide escape from an unbearable reality. One step towards ensuring that a dream becomes a realizable vision is to share it with others, just as Martin Luther King did, so that other people too can own and be motivated by it. But such sharing is not enough; progress depends on others taking ownership and taking action. This chapter examines how to move beyond the initial challenges (for example, identifying and engaging stakeholders, discussed in the last chapter), to the process of translating a shared vision into actions.

From dreams to visions: Three stories

Throughout this book we will use three stories to illustrate how to move beyond dreams, through visions and computer simulations, to actions. It is time to introduce these three stories now. Each of these stories seeks to illustrate different aspects of the process of moving from dreams to visions and actions. Although each of them tells a small part of a bigger story, they are also complete in themselves.

The River-maker

In the previous chapters we briefly encountered Rajendra Singh. It is now time for a proper introduction. Rajendra Singh's dream was to bring improved health care to rural people in India's desert state of Rajasthan. An Ayurvedic[2] physician and a government employee in an adult education project, Rajendra Singh gave up his job in the state capital of Jaipur in order to realize his dream in the village of Thanagazi, where at the time there was no groundwater. Thanagazi had declined to a mere shadow of its former status, as able-bodied inhabitants had fled the drought to earn their money elsewhere, leaving only the elderly, women and the very young. Those that remained behind relied on these emigrés for remittances. Life was hard, there was little food, and the only water available was muddy and involved a long walk. Despite these harsh conditions, Rajendra Singh and his four colleagues were allowed to stay and live in the local temple. In time he had gained the trust of the villagers and set up his dispensary while his colleagues began to work on adult education. It was only when an old man from the village, Mangu Lal Patel, bluntly told him that they needed water, not medicines or education that they realized they were delivering services that were not demanded. Their dreams were not being shared: a common vision did not exist.

Figure 3.1 Mangu Lal Patel
Source: Fergus Sinclair

The rest of this story is about how Mangu Lal Patel's dream came true with Rajendra Singh's help. Mangu dreamt that a landscape dotted with johads, traditional ponds for collecting and harvesting water, would help resuscitate a village dying of thirst. Together both men translated the dream into a vision by identifying the elements of the dream and turning them into a strategy, by developing an understanding of the present context (including the nature of the resources available and needed) and by being clear how they would know their vision had been achieved. Some 17 years after Mangu first shared his dream and Rajendra Singh began turning the vision into reality, the Ruparel river has begun to flow again, the Arvari river has been revived, and thousands of villages have water. The strategy was based on using traditional methods of water engineering and better farming methods supported by the collective action of local people who shared the same vision.

Previously we mentioned that these efforts had not gone unopposed. Clearly the vision was not shared by everyone; indeed initially it was shared by hardly anyone. It took Rajendra Singh three years to build his first johad: he dug it himself with the help of the elders and the women of Thanagazi village. These are the bare bones of the River-maker's story. As the book proceeds we will let this story unfold through the logic of our 'visions to action' process in order to illustrate this process. To make things perfectly clear we have recast the River-maker's story in the mould of the approach that we advocate, although Rajendra Singh did not use it himself. However, when we met in 2004, Rajendra Singh did say that our approach could have been useful in convincing at least the water engineers of the merits of their work. Several destroyed johads and many thousands of person-days of work could have been saved as a result.

Figure 3.2 Women commencing construction of a new johad
Source: Fergus Sinclair

Broomgrass collectors

In another dry part of the world, in Zimbabwe, Mrs Siwela had a very simple dream: she simply wanted to make enough money out of making and selling brooms to ensure that her family had enough to eat. That year the rains did not come and the crops failed. Her son Ramushe explained 'food has been difficult to get, even if one has money. That is why Mother is trading brooms for maize.' Mrs Siwela lives in the village of Batanai on the edge of the Mafungautsi forest in central Zimbabwe. She spends the dry

months of the year harvesting broomgrass,[3] and making and selling the
brooms that give the grass its name.
She is not alone in this; 15 other
households in her sub-village of
Mafa[4] are also engaged in this activity. They are the poorer households,
widows or single mothers, and people with marginal agricultural lands.
Making and selling brooms is an important economic activity as it brings
in cash, or provides an item that can
easily be bartered. Each broom usually brings in Z$8–10 in one of the
nearby towns[5].

Figure 3.3 Richard urging
the broomgrass collectors
to develop a vision
Source: Ravi Prabhu

When Richard Nyirenda first encountered the broom-
grass collectors he found a small group of marginalized people who were
concerned that some of their number were resorting to unsustainable harvesting practices, digging and uprooting the grass, instead of cutting it with
a sickle. Brooms made of uprooted grass were easier to sell as the roots at
the base help to hold the broom together. Brooms made of cut grass tended
to disintegrate as the grass slipped out of the binding at the base. Richard
was interested in working with Batanai village to see whether better collaboration and structured learning could help improve the way people used
the forest as well as improving their livelihoods. He decided to ask the
people at Batanai whether they would be interested in meeting together to
develop a vision for the resources they used. At first there was scepticism;
people felt that they knew what they wanted from the forest, knew how to
get it, and the only thing they wanted was to have easier and freer access
to forest products, if only the Forestry Commission that 'owned' and managed the forest would let them. After a few months people grew to trust
Richard and began to understand what he was trying to do, and they agreed

to try this exotic activity. Richard and his colleagues had spent much of the first few months trying to understand the diversity of demands, uses and groups in Batanai, just as he had spent time understanding the diversity of species and products in the forest. He knew it made little sense to ask everyone in the village to come up with a single vision, as there was just too much diversity for this to make sense. Recognizing that broomgrass, thatchgrass, honey and construction poles each had a rather distinct group of people associated with them, Richard suggested that each of these groups devise a vision for their particular product. Although each of these groups developed their own visions, our story is about the broomgrass collectors.

To help the broomgrass harvesters in Batanai with this rather exotic exercise, Richard and his colleague Tendayi worked with one of the members of this group, Mrs Mabhena, to develop her vision of the future. As they sat together on the sandy ground under the shade of miombo[6] trees in Mafa village to create their first joint vision of the future, Mrs Mabhena stood up to tell them in Ndebele[7] about her personal vision of the future. It was clear that most of the members of the group were enthused by her vision – the future she foresaw seemed promising, even exciting. Following Mrs Mabhena's lead, and using the structure that Richard suggested, the group spent the next two hours in intense discussion, formulating a shared vision, as illustrated in Box 3.1.

This visioning exercise was followed by several other activities designed to help devise ways to put these plans into action. These workshops focused on turning the visions into computer models that could give rise to simulated scenarios of the future. Some 20 members of the group worked with Richard and other colleagues to turn the vision into a computer model through a process that saw them drawing on a whiteboard their perceptions of the links between the natural resources they harvested, the desired future, the constraints to achieving this future, and the indicators they could use to measure their progress towards these goals. After they were satisfied that the resulting diagram represented their understanding of the vision and their interactions with the broomgrass resource, they went on to create a computer model (see Chapter 4), before examining selected

Box 3.1 Current and future scenarios

The scenarios developed by the group of broomgrass harvesters were
based around the current and desired future states of five key indicators,
which were closely linked to the strategies they had developed to bridge
the gap between the present situation and the desired future:

1 *Greater involvement* – the group wanted to increase participation
   from 15 households (mainly women from households close to the
   main road) to some 50–80 per cent of households in the resource
   management committee (about 375 households), with greater
   gender parity. Their expectation was that greater involvement
   would provide more opportunity for mutual assistance.
2 *Sustainable harvesting* – grass that was uprooted was easier to
   sell, but the group recognized this was unsustainable and wanted
   all harvesters to cut grass with a sickle.
3 *New markets* – brooms had been sold at dispersed markets,
   some far from home, incurring high transaction costs. The group
   planned to develop a market in the nearby town of Gokwe; by
   creating a quality product they would attract buyers to this local
   market.
4 *Consistent rules* – the 15 resource management committees
   surrounding Mafungautsi forest had different rules and had permits
   that were renewable daily. In future all RMCs would have the same
   rules and permits would be issued for longer periods of time.
5 *Greater profit* – group members earned around Z$15,000 annually
   from the sale of their brooms (net of costs),[8] and the group hoped
   to double this income. Based on these indicators and the strategy
   inherent in them, the broomgrass harvesters formulated an action
   plan that involved meetings, lobbying for influence and changing
   the statutes of the resource management committee. This action
   plan clearly identified responsibilities and had a set of indicators by
   which progress towards implementation could be monitored.

scenarios. These scenarios were simulated for two to three years into the future. Later in this chapter we will look at some of the key steps in the workshop process in order to understand how it took place. For the moment, a more important question is, did all this effort lead to any improvements?

To answer this question, let us return briefly to Mrs Siwela. Following the workshops, Mrs Siwela decided to add value to her brooms by binding her brooms differently and at the same time decorating them using polythene fibre. She found that the brooms sold quickly at five times more than ordinary brooms! This is quite astonishing; remember that brooms made of cut grass were being driven out of the market by brooms made of uprooted grass. Mrs Siwela has since displayed her beautifully decorated brooms at the Gweru Provincial Agricultural Show and has found it easier to barter them for food. She is not the only one in her user group to have switched to the new form of harvesting and processing (no longer uprooting grass); all the other members of the user group have followed her lead with equally good results, and the trend is catching on in other villages that surround the Mafungautsi forest. This simple insight by Mrs Siwela had important consequences for the livelihoods of many people. Because it was their own insight and initiative, the whole process of turning a vision into an action plan has not only brought about a change in behaviour, it has also given people a great deal of self-confidence and released initiative and energy. These were the same people who had to be persuaded to attend the training for transformation workshop run by Richard!

Resource sharing in Mafungautsi Forest

> 'Please' said one chief with a sad twisted smile
> 'your hacking is stretching for over a mile.
> These forests provide us with edible sap,
>   and cow berry fruits;
> not to mention the spirits that live in their roots.'

'Never fear,' barked McGee, 'our work does no harm.
It's your very own cutting that's cause for alarm.'

'Why cutting in chaos for your houses and fuel
wastes fine wood we could sell in ol' Liverpool.
If you keep using forests for your insatiable needs
how will we ever supply Europe with thneeds?'

Ode to the Lorax, Jesse Ribot[9]

In this parody Jesse Ribot nicely summarizes some of the resource use conflicts facing stakeholders in the Mafungautsi Forest, where there was disagreement about the extent and consequences of timber harvesting. Local villagers felt they had a right to harvest small trees for use as poles in house construction, and saw their harvest as harmless. Forestry Commission officials felt that these harvests were detrimental and wanted additional forest guards to stop the illicit harvest, not only of trees, but also of honey, as the practice of smoking bees was thought to cause wildfires. Concerns such as these stimulated a group of researchers to try to provide the tools needed to address these long-running arguments in a better way.

These researchers met in the Gwayi forest of western Zimbabwe in May 2000, seeking to devise tools to evaluate alternative forest policies and help identify strategies that were likely to be successful. Their proposal was to use FLORES (Forest Land Oriented Resource Envisioning System),[10] a framework for exploring policy alternatives across landscapes that could be adapted to various situations. Their first test of this framework in Indonesia two years before had shown that it was technically feasible for a diverse group of scientists to construct a simulation model of a forest margin landscape.[11] The next step was to see if local stakeholders could participate in developing and using such a model.

The FLORES researchers worked with a group of forest management professionals and researchers who were interested in finding ways to improve the management of Zimbabwe's Miombo woodlands, especially with respect to the collaboration of local communities in the management process. The group decided to try out the FLORES framework in the Miombo woodlands of Zimbabwe. Their efforts were driven by a vision of a forested landscape in which local people exceed their subsistence needs and escape their poverty trap, a legacy of history, geography and economic downturns. This vision foresaw these people supplementing food and cash earned through production and sale from agriculture – growing maize, cotton and vegetables as well as tending livestock – with cash earned from the sale of forest produce. They would achieve this without compromising the existence of the forest resources they depended on. So far this vision is no different from most other visions of sustainably managed forests (or other natural resources). What made this vision different was that this team wanted to achieve these goals through adoption of a strategy of adaptive collaborative management. Thus the big question was whether the processes of social learning, improved collaboration, better social networks and collective action would lead to better management of resources and people, and therefore help to reach the envisioned future? In other words, did it make sense to prioritize investments in social and human capital over financial, physical and natural capital? The researchers were engaged in a long-term programme of action research[12] with local communities around the Mafungautsi forest and this research offered an opportunity to experiment with computer simulations to explore this envisioned future. Could these simulations lead to new insights related to the research, the approach and activities? These were the questions that were posed to the FLORES group.

Attempting to answer these questions would mean trying to simulate conditions in and around the Mafungautsi[13] forest. This 82,000 hectare forest area had been chosen for the action research because of an existing policy experiment in collaborative management by the Forestry Commission. The Mafungautsi State Forest lies on a large plateau on the edge of the Zambezi Valley in Gokwe district in central Zimbabwe. It is

unfenced and surrounded by village communities. Some of these communities lived on the plateau before it was designated a state forest in 1954.
Many people live near the forest and make considerable demands on it for
fuel, construction materials and non-timber forest products. In the late
1990s, resource management committees[14] (RMCs) were established in an
attempt to solve conflict over forest resources. Communities participating
in RMCs have access to forest resources via an agreement between the state
and the villagers. The broomgrass collectors were part of this resource sharing experiment.

The Mafungautsi area is culturally diverse, as it is a
'new settlement' area. The first settlers in the Mafungautsi Forest area
were the Karanga-Shangwe people in the 1800s. With time the Ndebele,
Shona and Tonga have also settled in the area. Agriculture (mainly maize
and cotton) and livestock grazing are the dominant land uses. The forest is an important source of thatchgrass,[15] broomgrass, honey, mushrooms, insects (especially mopane worm)[16] and fruit. The area is also important as a catchment for Lake Kariba, as a World Heritage Area and
National Park, and for tourism and safari hunting (the 'big five', Cape
buffalo, elephant, lion, leopard and rhinoceros can be found in the
area). Some of the key management issues in the area relate to collaborative management, rural development and conservation (see Table 3.1).

Table 3.1 Selected issues, options and indicators identified by participants at the first
modelling workshop

Issue	Options for mitigation	Indicator of success
Forest clearing for agriculture	Improve productivity of existing farmland	Deforestation rate
	Alternative employment	Household income; school attendance
Unmanaged fire in forests	Add value to forest products	Health and nutrition
	Promote domestic bee-keeping	Fewer wildfires

Source: Synthesis of notes from Camp Selous break-out groups led by Fergus Sinclair and Robert Muetzelfeldt.

Participants recognized that human interventions are pivotal in shaping the nature of the Miombo, and documented a range of activities that may affect land cover in communal lands:

- clearing – cutting trees, burning felled trees and removing stumps;
- cropping – ploughing, planting, weeding, fertilizing (with forest litter, crop residues, manure, termitarium soil or inorganic fertilizer), protecting, harvesting, processing and selling produce;
- gardening – cultivating, planting, weeding, watering, harvesting, processing, selling vegetables and fruits;
- livestock – herding, collecting and storing stover (by-products from fields, for example, maize stems);
- collecting forest products – wood for fuel, construction wood, wild fruit (including honey and mushrooms), game, fibres, making items, selling products;
- household maintenance – collecting water, preparing food, maintaining infrastructure;
- maintaining social relations – meetings, brewing (beer);
- off-farm employment.

The vision of escaping poverty through sustainable resource use has been articulated above with broad brush strokes. Moving from this first vision to something more detailed was a slow process involving several workshops and a lot of thinking. These workshops were interspersed with periods of action research during which the vision 'settled' becoming clearer and more detailed. As a result the researchers had a better idea of who the actors were, how they might relate to each other and what avenues existed or might be created for learning and communication. This process allowed participants to understand what it was that they really wanted and how these concepts might best be expressed.

It became clear that the problem was an insidious one: in Mafungautsi there was no urgent problem waiting to be addressed – no forest that was going to be cleared for a mine or drowned by a dam, and there was no need for an impact statement or a cost-benefit analysis. No one was being evicted and no lives were threatened. Instead there was a forest surrounded by poor people who were slowly nibbling away at its edges without improving their economic or social condition. There was no acute illness that could be treated with emergency surgery or a wonder drug. Instead there was gradual, chronic wasting of people and resources at a level that by and large escaped public notice. The challenge faced in Mafungautsi is at the heart of development – how do we make sure that resource management does not result in palliative care of a moribund patient? How can we make sure that the patient recovers and has a good long-term prognosis? Emergency surgery and wonder drugs succeed only for a few patients. Most natural resource problems are chronic illnesses that receive scant attention and as a result there are scant resources available to help them. They have to help themselves as far as possible. Our vision of adaptive collaborative management suggests that this is possible.

Creating a vision

Visioning is a popular way of generating consensus among stakeholders about action plans for local resource management. By visioning we mean a facilitated process to generate a shared vision of the future. Our aim is to strengthen the link between visioning and the exploration of scenarios based on these visions using computer models. Our first step is to take a closer look at how to facilitate the development of a vision. Obviously there are many ways to go about creating a vision, and what we propose here is based on our experiences in several countries around the world.

One of the pioneers in system thinking and a scientist deeply concerned about the future of our planet, Donella Meadows,[17] once pointed out that a good vision:

- focuses on what one really wants, not what one will settle for (for example, really want: self-esteem, health, human happiness, permanent prosperity; settle for: fancy car, medicine, GNP, unsustainable growth);
- should be judged by the clarity of its goals, not the clarity of its implementation path;
- must acknowledge, but not get crushed by, the physical constraints of the real world;
- must be shared, because only shared visions can be responsible;
- has to be flexible and evolving.

Thus the process of envisioning is at least as important as the particular visions themselves. These five points form an important guide to the visioning process, if dreams are to be more than mere flights of fancy.[18]

The visioning process

The first step in a visioning process is to identify the group that should be involved in the visioning. We have dealt with this in the previous chapter, but remind you that the process involves identifying a problem or issue that is of interest and ensuring that all the important stakeholders have been invited to join the process. Once this has happened, the group can meet to start the process. The steps taken in visioning are as follows:

- Participants are asked to express their vision of what they want to see in future, especially regarding

changes in their village, local environment or lives, in
the foreseeable future (say two to five years from the
present).

- They are then given time to reflect on this vision and
discuss it among themselves.
- With the help of a facilitator they then use key words,
phrases or indicators that are clearly understood by all
to describe the current state of affairs and how they
hope to see it change in the future. They will try to be
as explicit as possible.
- Next they identify possible hindrances to and
opportunities for attaining their future or desired
scenario.
- After this they are asked to imagine how the vision
could be brought about and what will need to change
as well as what the implications of these changes
might be.
- Finally, based on these reflections and discussions,
they begin identifying and planning their actions (as
well as how they plan to monitor and learn from the
outcomes of these actions).

None of the steps mentioned above *needs* a computer. However, our experience with using computer-generated simulations to explore scenarios based on visions suggests that if the group involved has different interests within the same broad vision, and if the context within which the vision is being embedded is a complex one (that is, there are many factors or variables connected to each other in more than one way), then it can be very helpful to use computer simulations to explore scenarios.

We recommend the use of the five-role system of facilitation,[19] which involves a facilitator, a modeller, a recorder, a gatekeeper and a process coach:

- The *facilitator* guides the whole workshop process, prompting the participants to express their views and leading the teamwork in development of the vision and model. The facilitator is responsible for the social dynamics of the participants. This role is absolutely crucial for the success of the workshop.

- The *modeller* helps the workshop with the technical aspect of model construction, reflecting on the model as it is constructed by the team, and helping in particular with formalization of the model as a running simulation. The modeller must be very careful not to use his/her expertise in modelling to interfere with the model's conceptualization by the participants.

- The *recorder* makes notes throughout the workshop and helps with capturing the ideas, views and understanding expressed by the participants. Depending on how the facilitator wants to operate, the recorder may take on the role of 'scribe' in drawing the vision and model diagram on a flipchart or whiteboard. It is important to make sure that there is a way of capturing ideas and suggestions that are made whilst diagramming which are 'asides' or comments that should be recorded but not on the diagram itself.

- The *gatekeeper* is a go-between, focused on the participants, helping them to engage fully in the process. The gatekeeper usually belongs to the same institution or context of the workshop participants so she or he is an 'insider'. The gatekeeper's role is to liaise between the facilitators and the participants, checking that there is good understanding on both

sides and working to keep up the motivation of
the participants.

- The *process coach* is a sounding board for the
  facilitator, watching the group dynamics of the process
  and monitoring progress, participation and direction.
  They are usually an experienced facilitator themselves.
  The process coach should mostly reserve their inputs
  for private discussion and give suggestions to the
  facilitator during breaks, such as recommending that
  a silent person is brought into the process more, or
  suggesting a change in direction. The coach must be
  careful not to undermine the facilitator.

In some circumstances, it may not be possible to have five facilitators. In such cases, we recommend that these five roles nonetheless be recognized and shared amongst the facilitators. We do not advocate that the process is attempted with a single facilitator; the outcomes are too important to jeopardize through poor management of the process.[20] It is important that everyone has a chance to discuss and is comfortable with their roles before the workshop. As the number and diversity of participants increase, the importance of these five roles increases.

There are many advantages of a structured visioning process. It makes it possible to retrace one's steps at any stage to determine where a path might have bifurcated. It also makes it easier to take a whole group forward together to experience a sharing of ideas and thoughts. The software package 'Co-Learn' supports this process (available on the website and CD complementing this book – see page 143 for how to access these).

In the subsequent chapters we return to examine the details of putting the vision into a computer, quantifying the relationships, generating simulated scenarios and determining suitable courses of action.

The building blocks of visions

The process of turning dreams into visions begins with bringing together the people who need to share in the vision. The next step is to identify distinct elements that can guide the development of these visions into scenarios that can be evaluated and acted upon. Our experience with turning dreams into shared visions suggests that it is useful to think of visions being made up of the following elements: the *desired future*, the *current context*, *strategies* of how to get from the current context to the desired future, key *resources and influences*, the *actors* (people who are needed to help realize the strategy), and *indicators and levers* (things that you can change to influence progress towards the vision).

Before we take a closer look at these six elements, it is important to understand how we intend to use the three stories to illustrate different types of visioning processes. In the River-maker story, a few individuals were involved in the process of developing the vision, and the process of developing the vision was intuitive and evolutionary, rather than explicit and structured. The scale at which the vision was initially articulated was that of a small catchment area of a johad. The broomgrass story illustrates a case involving a group of people who followed a structured process of developing their vision using external facilitation in a relatively short period of time. In group processes such as this not all expectations and motivations are known, indeed some are deliberately hidden. It is an example of a process where a group of people is seeking to improve some aspect of their own livelihoods, focusing on a single resource on the scale of a *vlei*.

Finally we have the Mafungautsi story. Here again, a group of people followed a structured process to develop a vision. Unlike the broomgrass group, this group were not direct beneficiaries of the resources and visions. The scale was also quite different and encompassed several resources with competing interests at the landscape scale.

Desirable futures

The first step in turning a dream into a vision is to identify the desired future. In a narrow sense the desirable future is the original dream as shared among the group of people in trying to realize it. In the case of the River-maker it is Mangu Lal Patel's dream of clean water perennially available in the wells of his village, of villagers who do not need to migrate, and of crops that do not wilt when rain is scarce. He was surely telling Rajendra Singh a dream that was shared by all the people in the village. His dream was about a desired future in which the availability of a single resource had been changed. It was a simple, yet powerful dream that unleashed a tremendous amount of energy and action, once it was shared with the right people.

The purpose of visioning is to enable people to articulate their hopes and to empower them to think that it is possible to achieve them. Visioning is most effective when imaginations soar and people think freely about their desires for the future without feeling constrained by their knowledge of the present or by the expectations of others.

Context

When dreaming of a desired future, we may have our head in the clouds, but it is important that we keep our feet on the ground and deal with present day realities. The context recognizes the current situation, especially regarding opportunities and constraints.

In the River-maker story, the context recognizes that Thanagazi village in Rajasthan was afflicted by a drastic shortage of water and labour, and agriculture could not meet subsistence needs. It also reveals the presence of a social work project in the village, and the continued existence of traditional knowledge about water-harvesting systems. In addition, government efforts to provide water were invested in large irrigation projects with inflexible bureaucracy. These and other facts helped to pin down the present context clearly and concisely, and gave sufficient information about the situation to help us understand the difficulty and duration of the path to the future.

Strategies

A strategy is a plan to progress from the current context to the desired future. A useful metaphor is that of a pathway, or of a bridge if the 'gulf' between the present and the future seems vast. Mangu's vision was of a green village, where all generations were present and satisfied. Rajendra Singh's strategy was simple – to use Mangu's traditional knowledge about johads and any available labour to demonstrate that there was a way to achieve this vision simply and within the means of most villages.

The broomgrass harvesters wanted to ensure the sustainability of their resource by exploring other means of binding their brooms as well as by imposing better controls and by social chastisement of those who continued to uproot broomgrass instead of using a sickle to cut it. The vision of the researchers was to see forest resources contributing to sustainable paths out of poverty for rural folk, and their strategy was to use learning and collaboration to catalyse improved management.

Key resources and influences

In the River-maker story, the key resource was water. The resources available to Rajendra Singh were his labour and that of other village volunteers and the land for the johads. In the broomgrass case, it was the amount of broomgrass available in the *vleis* and of course labour, sickles and transport. In the ZimFlores[21] model, the resources include the forest, maize and cotton crops, grazing lands, vegetable gardens, livestock, labour and financial and social capital. Recognizing the key resources is an important step in making a vision more explicit, and transforming it from words into a more substantive form (as we will see in Chapter 4).

Another crucial step in making a vision substantive is to identify the key influences between these resources and other elements of the vision. An influence exists when one element can directly affect another element of a vision. For instance rainfall influences whether a johad fills and how fast broomgrass grows in a *vlei*. The process of documenting these influences often leads to new insights and sometimes contributes to important breakthroughs not previously anticipated.

As the broomgrass vision was being developed as a diagram and influences between elements of the vision were being drawn, a
lot of animated discussion took place among the people in the room. Who
would do the patrolling and enforcement of regulations? The members of
the government's Forest Patrol Unit were not very popular with the villagers, so should the resource management committee take this on? What
would their relationship be to the Forest Protection Unit? How would fines
be collected, who would keep them? Each of these questions resulted in one
or more influences being drawn. All this was fairly run-of-the-mill stuff –
after all the Forestry Commission had been trying similar approaches with
little success for years. Necessary yes, but a breakthrough? Probably not.
The group searched elsewhere for that breakthrough. The discussion shifted

Figure 3.4 Influences identified at an early stage of the ZimFlores model
Source: Jerry Vanclay

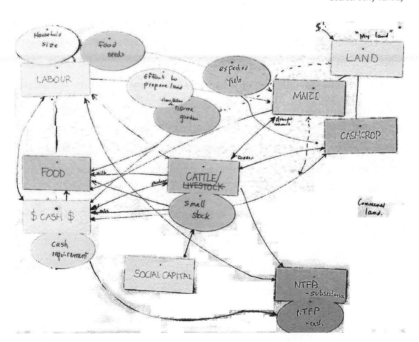

away from the resource to the final product, the brooms. Clearly if the brooms were tied differently they would not suffer from the rapid attrition suffered by most brooms made of cut grass and tied in the conventional manner. More variables were added, influences were drawn, and discussion continued. The manner of tying the brooms was seen as influencing market demand and clearly, market demand would influence the relative demand for uprooted brooms and therefore the sustainability of the resource. Suddenly, Lizwe Sibanda – one of the participants – suggested that it was not sufficient merely to think of tying the brooms in a better way, but necessary to go further, and to think of the overall *beauty* of the broom. At once, the room began to buzz with excitement. Here, possibly, was a way of not only undermining the uprooting and digging of broomgrass, but also of getting a better market price. The influences between these variables were drawn in and the vision process had taken an important step forward with a more effective strategy.

Actors

As we have said before, everything begins and ends with people. In the previous chapter we talked about how to identify the stakeholders, the people who have an interest in the opportunity or problem. Not all these stakeholders need to be active in contributing to realizing the vision, at least not initially. Therefore this element should identify the people and groups who are crucial to the realization of the vision in its simplest form. The work of Carol Colfer and her team offers some helpful guidance.[22] Naturally this group can and should be expanded as a vision becomes more challenging and more complex – as Rajendra Singh discovered through his fractured skull! It is important to avoid this pitfall of overlooking powerful stakeholders who may try to derail the process.

Indicators and levers

How do we know whether we have reached our goal? Obviously we need some milestones to indicate progress. These may be the number of days a well contains water in the dry season, the number of people returning to the village as conditions improve, the number of cut versus uprooted brooms sold in the market, or the health or income of an average household. All these milestones are called indicators – they are things that we consider important to monitor because they tell us about the degree to which we have achieved our vision. The challenge is to devise indicators that are both insightful and easy to measure. For instance, it may seem desirable to monitor the number of people returning to a village from provincial centres, but what does this really reflect? Can we be sure that people are returning because of an improvement in the quality of life in their village, and not because of an economic downturn in the provincial centre? Similarly, we may wish to monitor health of villagers, but it may be culturally inappropriate to survey villagers about the incidence of 'stomach upsets' or other afflictions. If indicators rely on answers to sensitive questions, they may not reflect the real situation. Such statistics that are hard to interpret unambiguously, or that cannot be determined reliably, are of little value as indicators. In contrast, the number of days per year that a well contains potable water is an indicator that is insightful and easy to measure.

Levers, as we all know, are things that we pull or push to make things happen that are far greater than the simple act of pushing or pulling. For instance, moving a lever a short distance may change the points on a railway track and change the destination of the next express train. So it is with our visions and the computer simulations. We imagine simple actions that may have a significant impact on achieving our goals. Rajendra Singh's case is a simple one in which there were few levers: his own labour and that of local villagers who had confidence in their traditional knowledge. The broomgrass harvesters postulated social sanctions and the development of new bindings as levers that would result in widespread behavioural change. In fact this behavioural change was further promoted when people realized that the material for binding the brooms was readily available in the strings of used synthetic fertilizer bags!

ZimFlores features more sophisticated policy levers such

as education, health care, forest patrols and commodity prices, but like the other levers we have considered, they remain concrete concepts that we can influence, and may have important consequences remote from the original initiative.

From visions to substance: Moving on

We will not dwell any longer on all the steps in the process of generating a vision. Instead, we encourage you to experiment with the materials included on the website and CD complementing this book (see page 143 for how to access these). The Co-Learn package is designed to help people understand how to successfully complete this process.

Having understood what a vision is and how to generate it using a facilitated process, we can now move on to exploring it using a computer. The steps in this process are described in the next chapters. The aim of this process is not to predict the future, nor to produce

Figure 3.5 A lever makes things happen, sometimes in remote times and places (railway on Dartmoor)

Source: Richard Knights

infallible plans. Rather it is to generate new insights, to explore options, and to gain confidence about our future course of action. The point of using a structured process and computer support is that these enable us to deal with situations too complex or long-term for us to imagine reliably. It is an important (and innate) skill to gloss over the details and reach a decision quickly; this skill is vital to human survival in emergencies. However, in many natural resource situations, the devil is in the detail, and it is prudent to use proven processes to explore as much of the relevant detail as possible. The tools that we illustrate offer a means to deal with the detail in a reliable way and to be confident in the conclusions that we draw. Such confidence may be built on the anticipation of a likely success, or more importantly, the knowledge that we could understand and recover from an unexpected, less desirable outcome. The next chapter illustrates how we can use a computer to explore scenarios, and to gain such confidence.

Notes

1   Dr Martin Luther King, address at Lincoln Memorial in Washington DC, 28 August 1963.

2   Ayurvedic medicine is India's traditional system of medicine, and is based on the prevention and treatment of illness through lifestyle intervention and natural therapies.

3   *Aristida junciformis* Trin. and Rupr.

4   The sub-village of Mafa has 194 households, so about 8% of households were engaged in broomgrass harvesting.

5   About US$0.50 at that time.

6   Miombo is a deciduous forest found in the seasonal tropics, and is dominated by trees of the genera *Brachystegia*, *Julbernardia* and *Isoberlinia* (all legumes

in subfamily Caesalpinioideae). Miombo woodland is the dominant vegetation of the central African plateau, extending from Tanzania and the Democratic Republic of Congo to Zimbabwe and Mozambique.

7   Ndebele is the language of the Ndebele people in Zimbabwe, but also often used by the Shangwe people in public.

8   About US$150 at the time of the workshop.

9   The prose is an extract from the parody *Ode to the Lorax* by J. C. Ribot (1997, Center for Population and Development Studies, Harvard University, www.ippnw. org/MGS/V5N2Lorax.html). *The Lorax* is a book by Dr Seuss (1971), in which the Onceler, a faceless narrator, chances upon a place filled with wondrous Truffula trees, which he greedily fells to produce and mass-market Thneeds. ('It's a shirt. It's a sock. It's a glove. It's a hat') The trees swiftly disappear despite repeated warnings by the Lorax (who speaks for the trees 'for the trees have no tongues'). With all the trees gone, hope for the future rests in the hands of the reader, who receives the last of the Truffula seeds.

10   Forest Land Oriented Resource Envisioning System: see J. K. Vanclay (2003) 'Why model landscapes at the level of households and fields?' *Small-scale Forest Management, Economics and Policy*, vol 2, pp121–134.

11   J. K. Vanclay, M. Haggith and C. J. P. Colfer (2003) 'Participation and model-building: Lessons learned from the Bukittinggi workshop', *Small-scale Forest Management, Economics and Policy*, vol 2, pp135–154. Also J. K. Vanclay (1998) 'FLORES: for exploring land use options in forested landscapes', *Agroforestry Forum*, vol 9, pp47–52.

12 Action research pursues action (or change) and
research (or understanding) at the same time,
cycling between action and critical reflection, and
continuously refining methods and interpretation as
understanding develops. See www.scu.edu.au/schools/
gcm/index.php?page_id=122&menu=5_137.

13 The name Mafungautsi means a 'place that smokes'.

14 Resource Management Committees are local-level
institutions charged with regulating the harvest of
minor forest products. Fifteen RMCs have been
created in villages surrounding Mafungautsi. Each
RMC comprises seven elected members who help
protect the forest area, issue permits, and collect
and invest permit revenue in projects chosen by
community members. Permits are issued for reeds,
broomgrass, thatchgrass and dead wood. Permit
fees are supposed to accrue to a community fund
to be invested in community projects. See E.
Mapedza (2005) 'Precaution in the designation and
management of forest reserves in Zimbabwe: the
case of Mafungautsi', in R. Cooney and B. Dickson
(eds) *Biodiversity and the Precautionary Principle: Risk
and Uncertainty in Conservation and Sustainable Use*,
Earthscan, London.

15 *Hyparrhenia hirta* L. and *Hyperthelia dissolute* (Nees ex
Steud.) Clayton.

16 Mopane worms are the larvae of the anomalous
emperor moth *Imbrasia belina* Westwood
(Lepidoptera: Saturniidae) and feed primarily on
mopane bush (*Colophospermum mopane* [J.Kirk ex
Benth.] J.Léonard). Mopane can make a significant
contribution to rural diets. See J. Stack, A. Dorward,

T. Gondo, P. Frost, N. Kurebgaseka and T. Taylor (2003) 'Mopane worm utilisation and rural livelihoods in Southern Africa' in *Conference on Rural Livelihoods, Forest and Biodiversity*, May 2003, CIFOR/INWENT/BMZ/GTZ International.

17   Donella Meadows (1941–2001), founder of the Sustainability Institute. www.sustainabilityinstitute. org/meadows/.

18   These six elements of a good vision are cited in R. Costanza (2000) 'Visions of alternative (unpredictable) futures and their use in policy analysis', *Conservation Ecology*, vol 4, art 5, www. consecol.org/vol4/iss1/art5/.

19   The five-facilitator approach is recommended by G. P. Richardson and D. F. Andersen (1995) 'Teamwork in group model-building', *System Dynamics Review*, vol 11, pp113–137. For more guidance on good facilitation of modelling workshops see J. A. M. Vennix (1996) *Group Model-Building: Facilitating Team Learning using System Dynamics*, John Wiley & Sons, Chichester.

20   Studies of participatory processes in resource management have shown that one of the main causes of failure has been a lack of a structure for discussion. M. A. Moote, M. P. McClaran and D. K. Chickering (1997) 'Theory in practice: Applying participatory democracy theory to public land planning', *Environmental Management*, vol 21, pp877–889.

21   ZimFlores was the version of FLORES created for the Mafungautsi context. See R. Prabhu, M. Haggith, H. Mudavanhu, R. Muetzelfeldt, W. Standa-Gunda and J. K. Vanclay (2003) 'ZimFlores: A model to

advise co-management of the Mafungautsi Forest in
Zimbabwe', *Small-scale Forest Management, Economics
and Policy*, vol 2, pp185–210.

22   C. J. P. Colfer, R. Prabhu, M. Günter, C. McDougall,
N. M. Porro and R. Porro (1999) *Who Counts Most?
Assessing Human Well-Being in Sustainable Forest
Management*, C&I Tool No 8, CIFOR.

4

Explicit visions

A picture is worth a thousand words. Words cannot capture fully the moment that a high jumper clears the bar, or that a chameleon snaps up a fly. Nor can words fully convey the information conveyed by a simple sketch map, drawn by a helpful stranger in a foreign land, to guide us to the train station. Pictures express our ideas clearly, universally and more immediately than words. Few of us are artists, and we cannot always photograph our ideas, but like that helpful stranger on the way to the station, we can all sketch ideas and visions in order to share them more fully, thereby turning them into blueprints that will ultimately guide our actions. So, in this chapter, we move from communicating with words to expressing these words in sketches and expressive diagrams, that can capture the essence of our vision clearly, like a well-drawn sketch map.

We want these pictures to be understood by all the people who have an interest in the issues involved, and to use them as a basis for developing quantified visions in the next chapter, so we need to develop and follow some conventions. These conventions help to ensure that our pictures convey meaning and are useful, making them much more than just pretty pictures.

Finding common ground

It is fashionable to use the concept of a road map to share visions about the future.[1] The concept is simple – a clear set of steps that need to be followed to reach a desirable future. There are two key features of these road maps that make them useful: they are explicit and they can be understood in the same way by the different people and interest groups involved, even if they disagree about their implementation. It is important that road maps are explicit; as Dennis Ross[2] said, 'You want to build a bridge to the future and the way to do that is to take the road map, which is right now a list of slogans, and turn it into something that could be the basis of reality.'

Box 4.1 Helping people to participate

Clive Lightfoot and Francisco Ocado[3] described their experience
with a participatory method developed in response to a lack of
progress with conventional technology transfer approaches. They
highlighted several steps:

- *Identify the Problem.* Ask farmers about their current topics
  of conversation, as this tends to be more productive than
  asking about problems directly. Canvass many topics to
  build an atmosphere of free exchange. Let farmers select
  topics to elaborate further. Group meetings are good to form
  consensus, but one-on-one in-field discussions are important
  to appreciate details.
- *Diagnose the System.* Establish the bio-physical causes
  and socio-economic constraints surrounding the problem.
  Draw diagrams, using a box for each issue, with arrows
  leading to a central problem. Discuss, and then redraw in
  concentric rings, with each box forming one segment of a
  circular diagram, with the size of each segment indicating the
  proportion of farmers responding to the point. Iterate, so that
  all participants develop the capacity to use the diagramming
  technique on their own.
- *Search for and Screen Potential Solutions.* Elicit farmers'
  priorities and ideas. Farmers have careful observations,
  important experience and constructive ideas that supplement
  formal research findings. Debate the 'pros' and 'cons', using
  the systems diagram to focus debate. If strong consensus
  cannot be reached on a well-defined test, go back a
  few stages rather than push forward with an unpopular
  experiment.
- *Define Hypotheses, Design and Conduct Farmer-led
  Experiments.* Visit individual farms and design experiments

on site. Plan measurements according to the information
needed by farmers and researchers. Get farmers and
researchers to visit plots together periodically to note
progress and take measurements.

- *Analyse Experiments.* Encourage participants to await final
  results and the testing of all hypotheses before relying on the
  trial, as early indications may be misleading.

This method encourages farmer participation and fosters the use
of systems logic in identifying problems, analysing systems and
elaborating experiments. Consequently, these experiments are very
different from typical cropping trials that place priority on maximizing
grain yield per hectare. Farmers may not be interested in immediate
increases in crop yield; their priority may be land rehabilitation and
saving labour. Participatory methods that use farmer knowledge
now help solve problems that conventional cropping research
was incapable of addressing. Participating farmers have increased
their capacity, skills and willingness to work together as a result of
working in this way. It also helps prepare them for farmer-to-farmer
training.

Source: This box is based on work by Clive Lightfoot and Francisco Ocado (FSDP-EV Project,
Department of Agriculture, Tacloban, Philippines), and published as Lightfoot (1987).

While the US President George Bush has attempted to facilitate change by
suggesting a road map to be followed by others, we advocate an approach
to natural resource management where the key actors themselves map out
the route. For this to be possible, we need to find some common ground,
to find a set of symbols that everybody can understand and use to map out
their vision. Just as cartographers have devised a set of standardized symbols
that assist a wide range of people to read maps, we will introduce some

symbols that encapsulate key aspects of the interaction between people and natural resources; symbols that have been found useful in many different contexts. The particular symbols that we have chosen are not the only ones that are available, but they are in widespread use, and have the advantage of directly leading to the quantification stage explored in more detail in the next chapter. These symbols will be introduced gradually as the story of making visions explicit unfolds in this chapter.

There has been a long and fruitful tradition of using pictures and symbols to assist communication about natural resource management. At the dawn of civilization, primitive people depicted hunting scenes on the walls of their caves. It is standard practice today for research and development workers to encourage rural people to sketch maps of key land and vegetation resources or to sit down with farmers in the centre of a village, scratching out causal diagrams with a stick in the dust, thereby assisting discussion of what contributes to the low and unreliable crop yields that they have been experiencing. A number of such participatory visualization techniques have been developed. Some of these methods lend themselves well to quantification – helping people to move along the continuum from a general idea to a clear image. This process of formalization often involves a series of steps that gradually accumulate detail about the natural resources in question, how people are currently using them, and how they envisage using them in the future.

In this chapter, we introduce the symbolic language with which we want to illustrate visions, and then illustrate how people have found these symbols useful to articulate, share and realize their vision. To do this, first we introduce key symbols through the story of the RiverMaker model, about Rajendra Singh's vision of perennial ground water in the dark zone of Rajasthan.

Representing knowledge

As we saw in the last chapter, Rajendra Singh, the River-maker, started with a single issue: people's need for clean water. Over time, as his work in Rajasthan unfolded, Rajendra's mission expanded to encompass river flows across the state. It is quite usual, especially in natural resource management, that the scope and focus of a vision will change as participants develop a better understanding of the situation. So it is with formal model diagrams. It is quite natural that these evolve and expand as we gain insights and understanding of the issues at hand. You will experience this firsthand over the next few pages as we develop the RiverMaker model and the diagrams get richer and more complete. It is useful to imagine a series of different views for different purposes, like photographs taken from different angles to reveal different aspects of a subject. We may end up discarding some pictures as we progress, even though we have learned something from developing them. Similarly, we may end up retaining several different images emphasizing different scales, different aspects of resources, and different ways that these resources are used.

Humble beginnings

Initially, the scope of Rajendra Singh's vision was small, encompassing water consumption in a single village. This involves a simple interaction between people in the village and how much water they draw from their wells (see Figure 4.1).

To illustrate this, we employ some simple diagrammatic conventions.[4] Resources in general, and in our case the amount of groundwater, can be visualized as the amount of the resource in a container. This container is referred to as a *compartment*. The compartment is represented in the diagram as a box (⬛). Compartments can be replenished or diminished by *flows* into or out of them. These flows are represented by arrows with a rate symbol[5] attached (⧖), and represent the flow of re-

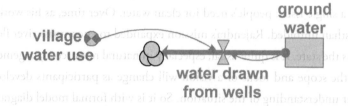

Figure 4.1 A simple grey model of groundwater extraction
Note: The grey colour (red on the computer) denotes that the model has been formulated, but not yet calibrated (that is, assigned the values necessary to complete the model.

sources, in this case, the rate at which water is drawn from wells by people in the village. So the amount of the groundwater remaining is reduced as people use water from their wells. Village water use is a *variable* that influences how fast water is drawn from wells. Variables are represented as checked circles (⊗) and they are connected to other elements by *influences* (⌒). The influence in this example indicates that the amount of water drawn from wells is determined by how much water is used in the village. In this example we do not need to know what happens to the water once it has been extracted from the wells, so the water flows into a *cloud* (☁) to indicate that it goes out of the system that we are modelling and is beyond our sphere of interest. Similarly, a flow may originate from a cloud, if the source of a resource flow is beyond our sphere of interest.

Our simple model diagram involves only three labelled components:

1   a compartment;
2   a flow from the compartment out of the system with an associated rate of flow;
3   a variable with an associated influence that determines the rate of outflow.

Even though the diagram is simple, it conveys a lot of information that can be quickly assimilated just by looking at it. Reading diagrams like this is intuitive because the symbols illustrate what is going on, and when we have drawn a diagram, we have already captured a lot of information about our vision.

You may have noticed that at this stage the model is grey (or red on your computer). This means that the relationships among the model components have not yet been defined.[6] We can see the structure of the model in terms of the components present and the influences between them, but we have not specified anything about how one component affects another. This is the subject of the next chapter but to help consolidate our understanding, we illustrate what happens when we do specify a model fully. We signal that a model component is fully specified by changing its colour from grey (or red) to black. In this example, if we assume that we start with 15,000 kilolitres of groundwater and that all the people in the village collectively use 30 kilolitres per day, then we have a fully specified model. When we run a simulation with this model, it shows that the groundwater is exhausted after about 500 days (see Figure 4.2). If the groundwater was not replenished, the village would enter what Rajendra Singh has described as a dark zone, where there is no groundwater available in the wells.

Many people find Simile and other system dynamics packages intuitive and easy to use, but those who find it more difficult may find that The Bridge[7] simplifies and assists with this task.

Figure 4.2 A simple model of water extraction with daily consumption of 30 kilolitres per day, and its simulation output as a graph showing groundwater levels over 500 days

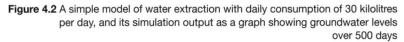
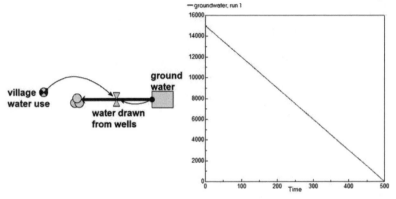

Embellishments

While it is good practice to keep models simple, the model illustrated in Figure 4.2 may be too simple to be of much use to anyone. Farmers like Mangu Lal Patel already knew that they were in a dark zone, with no water in their wells; they did not need a model to show this. But Rajendra Singh had discovered that they also had a wealth of traditional knowledge about the construction of johads, water percolation ponds that could be used to capture and store water when it rained. The stored water percolated slowly through the soil, replenishing the groundwater so that people could once again draw water from their wells. Rajendra began by working with people in one village to construct a single johad. To illustrate this, we need to expand our diagram. The most important addition is a compartment to represent the johad and a flow to represent percolation from the johad into the *groundwater* (see Figure 4.3). This captures the local knowledge about how johad*s* replenish well water. We also know that water harvest from the johad will depend on its *catchment area* and on the rainfall. The johad will also lose water through *evaporation*, which will depend on the water level in the johad, because more water means a larger surface area for evaporation. Finally, in this diagram, we have also shown that *village water*

Figure 4.3 Grey model of the first village johad

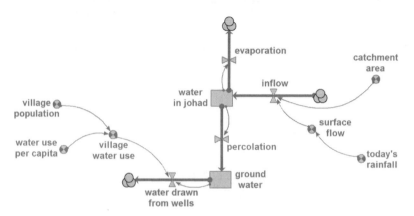

use depends upon the *village population* and on *water use per capita*. This is important since these two determinants of the village water use may vary independently of each other and may be important intervention points. For example, water use per capita is currently confined to domestic and livestock use, and may be expected to increase if there was sufficient water to irrigate crops and sufficient economic development for farmers to invest in technology to get water from tanks or wells to their fields.

This diagram is, of course, only one of many possible views of a village johad. A quick glance at the model, or a chat with local farmers, would reveal that we could easily add further complexity. This is both an opportunity and a potential danger. Rajendra Singh, for example, points out the importance of the soil's water retention capacity, so perhaps this should be a variable that influences percolation. We could add this to our model, but did not, because for this model (Figure 4.3) the soil type did not vary – it represented the actual soil in Bhikampura-Kishori village where the first johad was built. If we wanted to use our model to think about the performance of other johads on different soils then we would need to add this component.

Supporting structure

As models become more complicated they also become more difficult for people to understand. Models may become complicated because of the nature of their subject matter, or because of the number of relationships between components. In the latter case, the model can often be made more accessible by adding more structure, to make it easier for people to see at a glance what the model comprises. Several concepts are evident in Figure 4.3: the johad, the groundwater and the people in the village. We can im-prove our model diagram by collecting related model components within a *submodel*, denoted by a box (with rounded corners) that encloses the components (see Figure 4.4).

Figure 4.4 Grey model of the first village johad with submodel structure

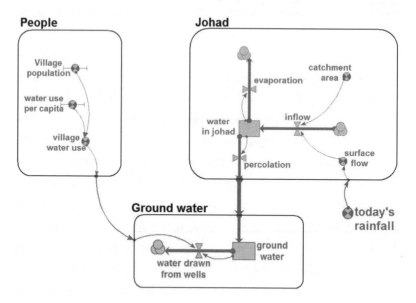

When you compare Figures 4.3 and 4.4 you can see that the imposition of a submodel structure has slightly altered how we perceive the same set of underlying symbols. You may have noticed that the submodels in Figure 4.4 are black, even though most of the model remains grey. This is because, as submodel structures, they are fully specified. Organizing our model in this way as a series of submodels has advantages far beyond making it easier to understand, as it allows us to treat each of the submodels as an object. Such objects may be assigned special properties, or can be used as models in their own right.

This flexibility, made possible by submodels, becomes important as the RiverMaker story unfolds and we want to picture many johads. The success experienced by Rajendra and the villagers after building their first johad led to construction of many more, and these not only contributed more groundwater, but also revived springs and rivers. Figure

Figure 4.5 Grey submodel of multiple johads extracted from the model in Fig 4.4

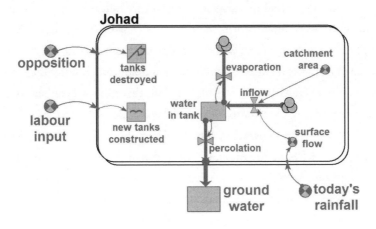

4.4 shows only one johad, but we can easily provide a mechanism to allow for any number of johads. Figure 4.5 shows the johad submodel, extracted from the model illustrated in Figure 4.4, and modified to become, not just one, but a number of different johads. We can think of this as a *population* of johads, indicated by the double lines around the submodel boundary; the multiple lines denote multiple instances.[8] Rather than having a constant number of johads, we want a picture that shows that new ponds can be constructed and that existing ones may be destroyed, so that the number that exists will change as time goes on. This is an important part of the system that we want to emphasize. Whenever we see these double lines of a population submodel, like this one for multiple johads, we look for components within it that control the number in the population. In this case, whether or not new johads are constructed[9] (⌇) depends upon having sufficient labour to construct them, while whether or not they are destroyed (╱), depends upon how much opposition there is to their development in the area – both of these variables are outside the johad submodel because they apply equally to all of the johads.

Once again, there may be circumstances where we would want to add more detail to our picture to capture different aspects of the system. If we were interested in the design of johads, for example, then it might be important to show that the size of johads can vary, affecting how much labour is required to build them and how much water they can subsequently harvest. But we will not explore that avenue here, and will conclude by adding the river to the model (see Figure 4.6).

We know that a johad only gets built if there is sufficient motivation and labour to construct one and that it may be destroyed if there is opposition. We can also see that the river runs across the landscape, receiving water from all johads, both through deep drainage and any overflows. Keen observers will note minor changes in the layout of the diagram; these are of no consequence as moving elements around has no effect on the functionality of the model, but merely affects the aesthetics. As with our previous views of the people and water resources in Rajasthan, this

Figure 4.6 Grey model of river flow with variable numbers of johads

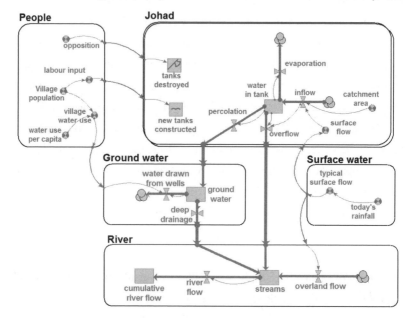

picture is just one of many possible pictures that we could draw. Much of the time, the local focus and action revolves around single villages, so this model is appropriate and is developed in the next chapter when we animate the model and use it to explore different scenarios. At the other end of the scale, there are also much larger water-harvesting structures, like the huge check dams that have been built with labour contributed from several villages. We would need to develop a different picture to encompass these efforts.

By now, our vision has come a long way, and evolved into a useful and explicit diagram that can form the basis for simulation studies. When we visualize a resource management issue and represent its context in a sketch or diagram, it is important to know where to start and when to stop. We need to be clear about the scope of what we intend to represent. The focal points that we start from, and the boundaries of our vision should encompass the perspectives of the people with whom we work. When we articulate a vision in words, even before we begin to convert it into a diagram, we already know a lot about it, but the process of developing a diagram helps to add rigour. Representing our model formally as a Simile model, using a standard notation, helps to clarify and communicate concepts. It has been our experience that this process of formalizing a vision as a model is an important step that helps to share the vision, to crystallize concepts, address oversights, evaluate its feasibility, and to progress towards an implementation plan.

Re-examining assumptions

The grey model portrayed in Figure 4.6 represents an important achievement in the transition from vision to action, but before we continue to calibrate the model (in Chapter 5), it is timely to review progress and to consider explicitly whether we have attained an appropriate scale and grain size (namely, whether the model is constructed from 'sand' or 'gravel'; more on this below), whether we have included all the variables necessary, and only the necessary variables, and whether we can adjust the structure of the model to make it easier to understand. We consider these aspects in turn.

Scale and granularity

Our discussion about Rajendra Singh and johads has not specifically addressed the questions of scale and granularity, but has gradually settled on both the temporal and spatial scales. In Figure 4.2, we calibrated our model to 30 kilolitres of water per *day*, and in Figure 4.3 we identified *today's* rainfall. In Figure 4.5, we included the catchment area of each johad and invoked a single river system. We have implicitly adopted a time step of one day, a spatial grain size of the johad catchment (in Figure 4.5 these need not be the same area), and a spatial scale of a river catchment. We have not identified a temporal scale, but there is a hint in the graph of Figure 4.2 that we are thinking of a model that runs for a few years (and not for a couple of days or for several centuries). While modellers often take these decisions about scale and granularity implicitly, it is appropriate to stop and question whether the implied scale and granularity are necessary and sufficient for the problem at hand.

In the case of our johads, we need to ask whether daily rainfall is adequate to estimate surface run-off within johad catchments and overflow from johads. Hydrological modellers might prefer to use hourly rainfall to model surface run-off for a specific soil type, but given our focus on the year-round availability of groundwater, such detail is probably unnecessary. It is certainly much easier to gather and use daily rainfall data, but is it necessary to use daily rainfall? Could monthly rainfall data provide a suitable basis? We have not specifically tested this, but our experience suggests that it would be hard to develop an adequate model of run-off and infiltration with monthly rainfall data (thus a daily time step is probably necessary). A daily time step is handy because it is conceptually convenient, because data are readily available at this scale, and because the model runs fast enough for our purposes at this scale.

Our decision to use the johad catchment as the smallest geographic unit arises from the knowledge that rainfall intensity, catchment area and johad capacity interact to collectively determine water storage and overflows. A coarser granularity (for example, dealing directly with the total number of johads within a river catchment) is unlikely to provide sufficiently accurate predictions. Conversely, a finer scale (for example, a model that explicitly identified each hectare of land) is likely to be cumbersome (for example, what to do with a one-hectare patch of land that straddles two johads?) and hard to calibrate (for example, we do not have sufficient soil data to adequately calibrate a model at this granularity). Thus it seems that the johad catchment provides an adequate and necessary spatial granularity.

The choice of an appropriate scale and granularity are important but context dependent, so while helpful guidelines can be offered, no hard-and-fast rules can be defined. Forest modellers have a 'rule of thumb' that it is useful to model three levels of scale, but no more. Thus models of tree architecture may model leaves, branches and the subject tree, and models of forest estates may model trees, stands (clumps of similar-sized trees) and the subject forest. However, experience has shown that there is no benefit in modelling plant growth at the leaf level if the scenario of interest is the forest estate: the small changes at the leaf level become irrelevant when aggregated to the estate level. Similar considerations apply for the time step: models of leaf-branch-tree interactions often deal with hours, days and years, whereas models at the tree-stand-forest level usually operate on an annual time step for time-frames of several decades. This experience from tree growth modelling appears to be generic and applies to many modelling endeavours. It is desirable to choose a granularity that contributes to a model structure that is easy to understand, that facilitates calibration, and that is substantially less (for example, about three levels, but not more) than the scale of interest.

Key resources and influences

The concept of 'necessary and sufficient' that we discussed with regard to the granularity and scale of the model also applies to the inclusion of variables and influences in the model. As Albert Einstein[10] remarked, a model should be as simple as possible, but no simpler. The challenge is to make a model:

- easy to understand,
- practical to use, and
- efficient to run, while
- maintaining enough realism to ensure
- reasonable predictions and
- retain the confidence of users.

As before, there are useful guidelines, but few hard-and-fast rules. Again, it is useful to draw on the experience of forest growth modellers to illustrate some of these guidelines.

Plant growth models come in a wide range of flavours ranging from the simplistic to the sophisticated, but the most complicated tend to be the least used. Some models make detailed calculations about the ability of light rays to reach individual leaves; while this demonstrates the mathematical skill of the modeller, it does little to improve the ability of the model, and most users do not care for such finesse. Similarly, we all know that soils can greatly influence tree growth, but most forest growth models do not require detailed soil data as an input to the model, simply because such data are too difficult to obtain, and asking users to provide it effectively precludes use of the model! Clearly, as we re-examine and revise a model, we should bear in mind the needs of the users of the model, and make sure that it meets their needs. This may mean culling parts of the model to foster understanding and ease of use.

Some years ago, the University of Melbourne[11] facilitated a discussion between a diverse group of modellers. One horticultural modeller advocated that a plant growth model should simulate all aspects of plant growth starting from the basic chemistry of photosynthesis. A forest modeller did some quick calculations and responded that with the computers of the day, such a simulation would run slower than the forest would grow, and would thus be useless for prediction. Clearly, if a model is to be used in an interactive way, it needs to provide a result within a reasonable time-frame. This may dictate limits on the complexity of the model, especially in models designed to operate at the landscape scale, and in those designed to simulate several decades. Such models require special consideration of the granularity and of the number of variables involved.

Most models are constructed to help stakeholders make decisions, so it is important that stakeholders have confidence in these models. Such confidence can be fostered by helping users to understand the model, as well as by demonstrating the quality of its predictions.

Communicating clearly

We began this chapter with an analogy to photographs and maps, and it is helpful to continue this analogy here. The difference between a carefree snapshot and a professional photograph is often not the content, but the composition. Similarly, a key difference between a quick sketch-map and a cartographic product is not the content, but the way in which the information is presented. Thus it is with models: careful attention to the layout may not alter its functionality, but can make it much easier to understand. We illustrate some general principles by drawing on the broomgrass example.

Figure 4.7 illustrates the initial concept for the Broom-Grass model, as drawn on a whiteboard. This representation is reproduced from an early stage of the brainstorming process, so it reflects thinking at that early stage of the process, before it was refined through evaluation and re-examination.

Figure 4.7 Whiteboard model developed by the broomgrass collectors

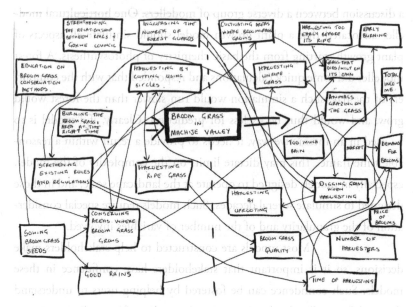

Figure 4.8 Simile model constructed by the broomgrass collectors

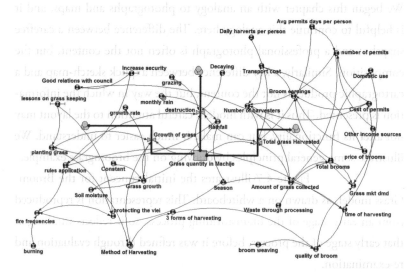

The broomgrass collectors, assisted by our colleagues Richard Nyirenda and Wavell Standa-Gunda,[12] developed this understanding into a Simile model. Their model (see Figure 4.8) is not so different from this whiteboard model. To the accomplished modeller, their model is unsophisticated and untidy, but it was nonetheless sufficient for the broomgrass collectors to explore alternatives, gain the confidence to implement their 'best bet', and to change their land-use traditions and livelihoods for the better.

Figure 4.9 illustrates the same model, after some tidying up by the authors. The functionality of this model remains much the same as in the model of the broomgrass collectors (Figure 4.8), but the layout has been changed to make it more accessible to readers. This has been done without consultation with the broomgrass collectors, so they may no longer recognize it as their model, but the functionality remains similar, and most of the parameters and equations embedded within the model's variables remain the same. The advantage of rearranging a model in this way is that it makes it more accessible to the uninitiated. In Figure 4.9, readers can see at a glance (from the submodel names) that the model addresses grass

Figure 4.9 The Broomgrass model after tidying up by an experienced modeller

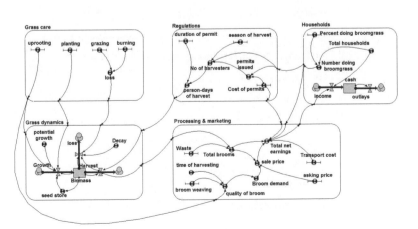

dynamics, regulations, processing and marketing, and so on. A simple rear-rangement of the model to reduce the number of criss-crossing lines, and to group related themes into submodels with helpful names, does much to make the model more accessible. This model is available from the website or CD that support this book (see page 143 for how to access these).

In the next chapter, we consider how to bring such a model to life by quantifying the relationships and preparing it so that it can be used to explore alternatives.

Notes

1   For instance, President George W. Bush's 2003 road map to peace in the Middle East; see www. whitehouse.gov/news/releases/2003/03/ 20030314-4.html.

2   Dennis Ross, special Middle East coordinator in the Clinton administration, as reported in *The Jewish Week*, 26 August 2005. See www.thejewishweek.com/ news/newscontent.php3?artid=11303.

3   This box is based on work by Clive Lightfoot and Francisco Ocado (FSDP-EV Project, Department of Agriculture, Tacloban, Philippines), and published as C. Lightfoot (1987) 'Indigenous research and on-farm trials' *Agricultural Administration and Extension*, vol 24, pp79–89.

4   Our diagrams use conventions drawn from compartment-flow modelling or system dynamics, a standard notation used in many modelling packages.

5   The rate symbol is an engineer's notation for a tap or valve.

6   The notation is generic to all system dynamics,

but some extensions (e.g., the colour convention) are specific to Simile, a powerful system dynamics modelling environment from simulistics.com

7   The Bridge software package is available on the website supporting this book, at www.cifor.cgiar.org/RealizingFutures.

8   This convention for multiple instances is not generic system dynamics, but is specific to Simile. Readers who wish to learn more about these and other extensions are advised to consult R. Muetzelfeldt and J. Massheder (2003) 'The Simile visual modelling environment', *European Journal of Agronomy*, vol 18, pp345–358.

9   A bird symbol is used, because the construct was originally developed to denote migration, i.e., a certain number of new individuals joining a population.

10   Albert Einstein (1879–1955), physicist, pacifist and humanitarian, widely regarded as the greatest scientist of the 20th century, awarded the Nobel Prize in Physics in 1921 (see http://nobelprize.org/physics/laureates/1921/einstein-bio.html).

11   J. W. Leech, R. E. McMurtrie, P. W. West, R. D. Spencer and B. M. Spencer (1988) *Modelling Trees, Stands and Forests*, School of Forestry, University of Melbourne, Bulletin No. 5.

12   W. Standa-Gunda, T. Mutimukuru, R. Nyirenda, R. Prabhu, M. Haggith and J. K. Vanclay (2003) 'Participatory modelling to enhance social learning, collective action and mobilization among users of the Mafungautsi Forest, Zimbabwe', *Small-scale Forest Management, Economics and Policy*, vol 2, pp313–326.

5

Substantive Visions

Eadweard Muybridge, *Gaits of the Horse*[1]

Moving from an outline to something of substance is never easy. Visions expressed in words and diagrams offer useful insights, but it is much more useful to have a functioning model that can be used to explore options and implications. Though these representations are similar in some ways, there is a substantial difference. The difference is like reading a comic strip in a newspaper or watching the same character animated in a cartoon. The experiences are immeasurably different. But the effort required to deliver a cartoon movie far exceeds that needed to sketch a comic strip. In the past, this daunting effort has been a major obstacle, hindering the development of simulation models able to help quantify visions. Fortunately, this situation is changing rapidly. New software, better hardware, established design principles, and a wealth of experience contribute to make it relatively easy to move from the grey model discussed in the previous chapter to a fully-fledged simulation model that can be used to explore alternatives. Moving from the static comic to an animated cartoon is what this chapter is about.

The model achieved at the end of Chapter 4 is like the script of a play, or the snapshots on the dust jacket of a DVD. This chapter involves getting the computer to 'run' our model, in the same way that actors rehearse a play, so that the director can make amendments to deliver the desired performance. In Simile, we do this by pressing the *run* button, a triangular button just like the play button on a DVD player or other electronic appliance (see Figure 5.1).

Figure 5.1 The run button on the Simile toolbar

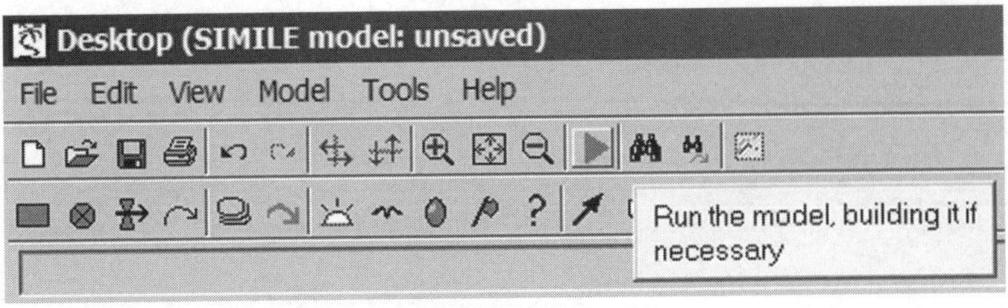

Bringing a model to life in this way involves fine-tuning it to a given situation by describing the states of the various components of the model, quantifying the relationships between them, and evaluating the behaviour of the model as a whole. These three steps are repeated until model predictions seem reasonable, both in terms of the logic embedded in the model, and in terms of the predictions made. Let's look at these steps in more detail.

Describing states

People share their observations and experiences through descriptions. A child can offer an insightful description of their favourite cartoon characters, commenting not only on their physical appearance, but also on

Figure 5.2 A small johad at Gopalpura, Rajasthan
Source: Fergus Sinclair

their behaviour. The challenge for modellers is to harness this intuitive skill by encouraging storytellers to become more specific so that the essential details can be incorporated in a model. The intuitive response is to add detail by resorting to analogies or word-pictures ('eyes as big as saucers'). Such illustrations can be helpful, but the real challenge is to draw out the description to get specific details. Fortunately, it is quite natural for storytellers to offer this level of detail when interacting with an interested audience. For instance, when asked in an interview 'What does a johad look like?' Rajendra Singh[2] responded, 'Imagine a semicircular pond, collecting the run-off from the tiny streams and rivulets in a much wider area. Our first one was about 5 metres deep, with an area of between 100 and 200 square metres, and a catchment area of 100 hectares …'.

This description provides much of the detail needed to initialize a simulation model of the rehabilitation of the Ruparel River basin. However, not all the johads had these dimensions (for example, the johad at Lava ka Baas was 14 metres deep and 200 metres long),[3] and we want the flexibility to vary the size of johads to see how their size influences their performance. This is easily done in Simile: pressing a button marked *variable parameter* creates the flexibility to vary these values when the model is run (see Figure 5.3). In this example the slider allows us to vary both the area and depth of the johad each time the model is run (or

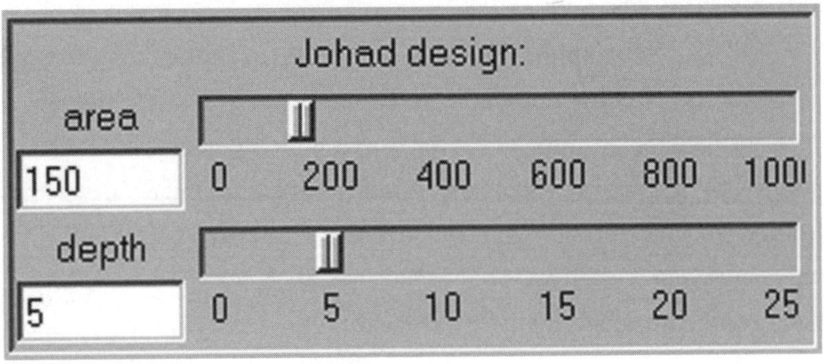

Figure 5.3 Slider to allow size of johads to be varied during simulations

even during a simulation), in much the same way as we vary the volume and tone controls on a radio to adjust the sound according to the content and context.

As we have seen in Chapter 4, modelling environments such as Simile make it easy to construct models. It is equally easy to enter the numbers to prepare a model for running simulations. One simply enters the appropriate number or equation and presses 'OK'. Details of how to do this are given elsewhere.[4] Here, we simply observe that the mechanics of entering numbers is trivial, and we turn our attention to the issue of choosing the appropriate numbers.

Quantifying relationships

Static objects like johads are comparatively easy to describe and measure, but these comprise a small part of most models. As we know, most models deal with the relationships between objects, and with motion and action. These aspects are amenable to description, but narratives are often qualitative rather than quantitative. Such descriptions inform modellers of the nature of the dynamics involved, but usually do not help to quantify these relationships. However, there are other ways to get at the information required. Typically there will be three ways to establish these dynamic relationships: the key relationships may be known already; it may be possible to measure the required relationship directly; or observed outcomes may be used to infer the underlying relationships.

Consider, for example, a group of young boys throwing stones at mangoes hanging out of reach in the tree overhead. The movement of their stones through the air is well understood and has been enshrined by physicists in standard formulae. These formulae[5] are neither known nor understood by the boys, who are nonetheless accomplished at throwing stones to achieve specific objectives, such as to retrieve ripe fruits from mango trees. Scheming for a stone to strike the stem of the mango at the right place with sufficient momentum to shake it free, and to be in the right place to catch the mango before it strikes the ground, involves complex calculus, but is done intuitively by boys who draw on their experience, and who use trial-and-error to improve their performance. Precisely the same principles are applied in using 'best guesses' to calibrate a model, and in fine-tuning the model on the basis of observed outcomes. In the case of the trajectory of a stone, this is rather contrived, but with many real world models it is a realistic and appropriate way to calibrate a model.

Picking mangoes in this way is so intuitive that a computer model would not be of much help; such models are normally reserved for more complex calculations. However, if we decided to build such a model in Simile, we would need to inform the computer about the path travelled by the stones. This process is known as *calibrating* a model. We could calibrate the relationships describing the trajectory of the stones in two ways: we could provide the standard formulae, or we could input a sketch representing the trajectories that we observed.[6] In the latter case, the sketch would describe the nature of the relationship, and we would need to make some observations of the height reached and distance travelled by the stone to fully calibrate the relationship. Just as the boys improve their aim through trial and error, feedback can be used to correctly calibrate a model. If at first, the model overestimates, the parameters that we guessed can be adjusted until predictions match our observations.

RiverMaker

As we have shown in Chapter 4, there are many ways that the RiverMaker model can be formulated, and no one way is better than other ways in every respect. However, a good representation should align with the way we think about the environment and should be amenable to calibration and testing. When Rajendra Singh talks about his work, he talks about people, johads, groundwater and rivers, so these are all useful constructs to use as submodels. Calibration starts with the *surface water* submodel, because it

Figure 5.4 Simile representation of the RiverMaker, showing detail only for the surface water submodel

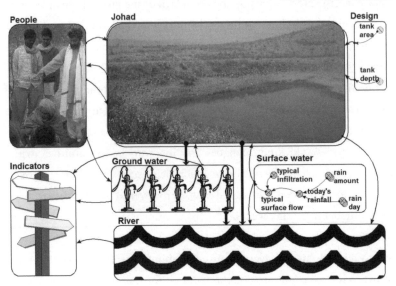

is not dependent on any other submodel (all arrows exit and none enter; see Figure 5.4) and could be run easily as a stand-alone model.

The model simulates the number of rain days each season, and the expected rainfall on each of these days (*today's rainfall* in Figure 5.4). A few trials allowed us to fine-tune the submodel to obtain a realistic annual rainfall distribution and amount[7] (570 millimetres) over a ten-year simulation. Notice that a few embellishments have been made to the model since Figure 4.6; it is quite normal to enhance a model in this way during its development. Once the rainfall was calibrated, the next step was to adjust the variables *typical infiltration* and *typical surface* flow to achieve a long-run average surface flow of 35 per cent of the rainfall, as reported by the International Water Management Institute (Sharma, 2002).[8] The variable *typical infiltration* did not need to influence percolation because we know that before the construction of the johads, Thanagazi was a dark zone with no groundwater.[9] At this stage, calibration of the surface water submodel was complete and our attention could turn to the next submodel, the johad submodel.

Several publications[10] give the surface area, depth and
catchment area of typical johads, and these data can be used directly in the
johad submodel. Evaporation is assumed to vary throughout the year, with
a low of 5 millimetres per day during the cool month of January and reach-
ing a high of 15 millimetres per day during the dry heat of June.[11] However,
to estimate the volume of water evaporated, we need to know the surface
area of the johad, which varies according to the depth of water. It is rather
complicated to model the volume of water evaporated directly from the
volume of water in the johad, and it is much easier and more transparent to
use some intermediate variables such as *current surface area* and *water depth*
(see Figure 5.5). The assumption that a johad approximates the shape of
an inverted pyramid (Figure 5.6) makes these calculations straightforward,
particularly when the intermediate variables are used. Notice that when the
water depth is half full, its surface area is one-quarter and its volume is one-
eighth of the capacity when full. These geometrical relationships provide all
the information needed to calculate all the intermediate variables.

Figure 5.5 Detail of johad submodel showing the use of intermediate variables

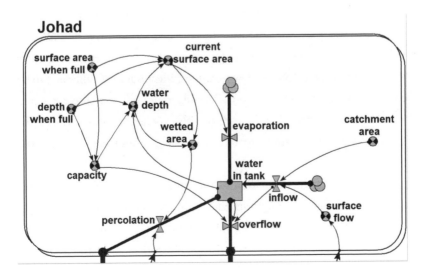

Figure 5.6 Diagram showing johad represented as an inverted pyramid

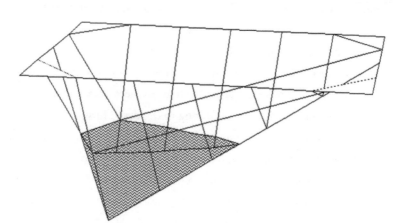

The calculation of percolation was facilitated by the use of these intermediate variables, but was hampered by the lack of any data on percolation rates. Fortunately, several observations provide a good basis for calibrating the johad submodel. Rajendra Singh[12] reported that water remained in the first johad at Bhikampura-Kishori for three months following the end of the monsoon; and Richard Mahapatra[13] reported that the johads reduced run-off from 35 per cent to 10 per cent and increased infiltration by 20 per cent . In the nearby village of Tolawas Mala, the first johad held water for three months after the first monsoon, for six months following the second monsoon, and three years after completion held water throughout the year.[14] With a few iterations, the model was calibrated to be consistent with these observations. This illustrates how a well-constructed model can be calibrated and checked with experiential observations, just as a boy can learn to throw a stone at the stem of a mango through trial and error.

The calibration of the RiverMaker model was completed by making some assumptions within the *groundwater* submodel to get reasonable patterns for the water in the wells. The resulting model is not necessarily 'right', but it appears reasonable and offers predictions that are consistent with observations at several levels of scale.[15] This illustrates that personal experiences, casual observations and other easily-obtained data can be used to calibrate models, especially when diverse observations from different sources can be used to confirm these inferences (this is often called triangulation).

In this fashion, we proceed step-by-step through each submodel, calibrating and testing each in turn and in concert, until we are satisfied with the overall model representation and performance.

ZimFlores

It is often easier to calibrate models involving objects and physical processes than to deal with models of people and communities, but the same principles apply. ZimFlores is of interest in this regard because the focus is the interaction between many people and diverse natural resources at the landscape scale. As we have said before, ZimFlores was not designed to solve a single acute problem, but rather to explore complex interactions of many chronic problems and to ensure that resource management finds a 'cure', rather than simply providing palliative care. As a result, the model becomes more complicated and requires a broader skill base to complete and calibrate.

The solution to these complications is idealization, and much of the challenge in formulating ZimFlores involved finding effective idealizations.[16] The implementation of household decision making relies in part on the notion of household wealth. This seemed straightforward during the early stages of model formulation, but our attempts to initialize this part of the model revealed some difficulties. Household wealth encompasses livestock, maize and earnings from cash crops, in an environment where many transactions involve barter, during a period of high inflation.[17] Our idealization was to record household wealth as 'dosh', the 'daily ordinary subsistence needs per household'. This seemed to find a suitable balance between oversimplifying and drowning in detail. Another issue was

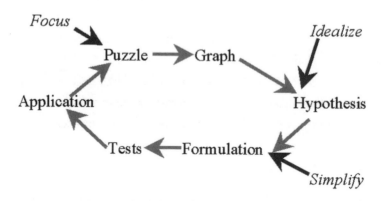

Figure 5.7 The modelling cycle showing where it is important to focus, idealize and simplify

the units to use for passing information between submodels. Initially, crop modellers requested a wide variety of specific detail, including, for instance, the amount and analysis of fertilizer applied. We resolved that our idealization should be to express everything as person-hours spent doing an activity selected from a standardized list. Idealizations such as these are crucial to the completion of a landscape-scale model such as ZimFlores; without them, attempts at calibration get bogged down in details that often make no perceptible difference at the landscape scale.

Figure 5.7 illustrates some key steps in the process of model idealization and formulation. We started by identifying a puzzle, establishing why we need a model. In many contexts where the aim of modelling is learning, the trigger is a puzzling issue, and hence the term 'puzzle' is used here as shorthand for the concept. This is a crucial stage, especially when large groups are involved, because success requires that all participants gain a clear view of a common puzzle. In the ZimFlores case there was more than one puzzle: was it possible to manage the natural resources in this landscape sustainably? Would adaptive collaborative management (that is, focusing on social learning and collective action) be the right strategy? Finding a common puzzle helps the modelling team to move forward in a 'joint enterprise'[18] in which they develop a common understanding and possibly a common 'language' for their project. A clearer view of the puzzle at this early stage (that is, a sharper focus) makes the rest of the process easier.

Having agreed on a puzzle, it is helpful to sketch simple graphs of the changes in key system variables over time to begin eliciting the team's knowledge about the system being modelled. It is also a way of encouraging more specific statements about the puzzle. These graphs or sketches anticipate the behaviour of the model and are extremely useful for model testing and for reflecting on learning later on in the modelling process. In the ZimFlores case the team did several things – they devised small strategy games using cards to map out how decisions and choices might be made, they drew maps of how they thought new information reached the village, and designed an experiment to test this. At this stage, the emerging model is an explicit representation of a shared understanding and can be thought of as a hypothesis about the system. Further development of this hypothesis requires specific details of key concepts to resolve the puzzle, to test the theory, or to understand and solve the problem. Generating the hypothesis is thus a process of conceptualizing. The next steps involve formulating the model in Simile (or some other explicit form) and testing it. The ZimFlores model took shape on a whiteboard in a workshop setting, and it was relatively easy to translate it into a grey Simile model. Getting a model that could run was a much slower process as each relationship was discussed, debated and, where there were still doubts, tested during the process of quantification and specification. Finally, the model was used to see what light it shed on the puzzle. Often, the first attempt to use the model reveals inadequacies in the model and misunderstandings in the conceptualization of the puzzle, so it is appropriate to repeat this cycle (Figure 5.7) several times. In this way the modelling process becomes a learning cycle.[19] We have found that many rapid cycles[20] can be more insightful than slower, more measured progress, but such rapid cycling is not always possible with participatory modelling because time is needed for knowledge to be shared between participants and for participants to gain an understanding of the model. The bigger the group and the bigger the model, the slower the cycles tend to be.

Another important idealization in ZimFlores related to rights to use land (rather than ownership). At one point during the evolution of ZimFlores, we discussed the many different forms of land-use rights. Many people will be aware of the relatively simple situation where the land is owned by the government, leased by a company, share-farmed by an individual, with the fishing and hunting rights owned by other parties. In Mafungautsi, the possibilities are even more complex. In theory, it is possible to implement this rich complexity in a Simile model, but we found that it was not desirable to do this. Instead, we chose to implement just two forms of land tenure: land owned by individual households and common land available for all to use. This has proved to be an adequate idealization and is easy to implement in Simile, which provides a construct to represent an association between two submodels.

Figure 5.8 illustrates one way to implement a tenure association between a variable number of people and a fixed number of land titles. Each *person* has a *name* and each piece of *land* has an *address*. A *title office* maintains a *register* with a person's name and the address of their land. *Rights* are an understanding between people that access is possible only when it is consistent with information in the title office register. The

Figure 5.8 Example of land tenure implemented in Simile

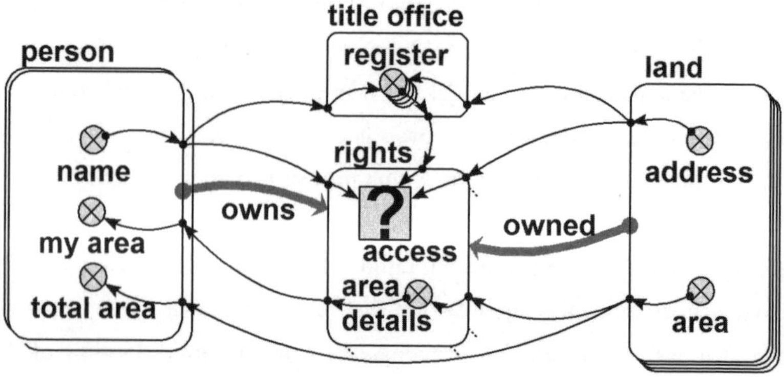

conditional submodel (rights) contains a test (access) that may be true or false; a person can only gain access to land if the result is true. In this case, access contains the simple statement that the register entry for this land (*address_owned*) is my name (*name_owns*). When this statement is true, a person has access to the piece of land. Thus when an influence comes directly from the land, a person 'sees' the total area of all the land. But when an influence comes via the rights submodel, a person only 'sees' land on which they have rights (denoted *my area* in Figure 5.8). In ZimFlores, the statement is a little more complex because it recognizes common land as well as private holdings. In Figure 5.8, the only form of tenure is full ownership, but a wide variety of tenure relationships is possible.[21]

ZimFlores was calibrated during a series of participatory workshops involving brainstorming sessions that focused on getting 'ball park' estimates (correct only to an order of magnitude) for the many parameters needed.[22] Initial estimates for these parameters were provided by a wide variety of local experts during a facilitated brainstorming session. These parameters were not embedded within the Simile model, but were provided via a separate parameter file so that they can be updated easily with standard text editors. The initial estimates were subsequently refined by rigorous cross-checking against published material and the views of other experts. Finally, the trial and error approach was used to make sure that the completed model could reproduce what we observed in our specific case studies.

This sounds straightforward enough, but this point is not reached without effort. When team members saw the first ZimFlores outputs during one of the workshops, there was nervous laughter: the outputs were demonstrably wrong. A few hours later, with a few new variables and some careful recalibration, we had plausible results for some of the situations that we had observed. However, further simulations by team leaders revealed other weaknesses in calibration, and it was only later that ZimFlores reached a stage that all participants considered satisfactory. The message here is that sometimes calibration can be participatory, but that calm, considered review remains an important part of the calibration process. An important part of this review process is to have someone manage quality control, to check every component of the model for consistency and documentation. The US space agency NASA has experience that illustrates the importance of such rigorous quality control. The Mars Climate Orbiter[23] crashed on Mars because one team of engineers was working in imperial units (feet and inches) and the other was working in metric, and the two teams did not share this assumption. More recently, the Genesis mission crashed on return to Earth because all four switches to actuate the parachutes were installed upside down.[24] Good communication between project teams, complemented with careful quality control, is crucial for success!

Despite this slight difference in approach, final calibration of ZimFlores proceeded in much the same way as for the RiverMaker model. Submodels with the fewest dependencies were calibrated first, tested as stand-alone models, and gradually the model was improved from a rough outline with 'best guesses' to a system with defensible parameters and behaviour consistent with our understanding and experience. It is impossible to attest that the model is correct, but we can assert that the model gives predictions consistent with observations made in the village, and behaves in a reasonable way when pushed to extremes. The danger of getting the right result for the wrong reasons has been minimized by focusing the model on our understanding of the system, rather than by seeking a simple 'best fit' to the data available. The resulting model is sufficient to explore many scenarios and to stimulate the discussion about how to realize our visions.

Evaluating Model Behaviour

The third stage of bringing a model to life is an evaluation of its behaviour as a complete system. Some view this as a 'reality check', an explicit test of the assumptions in the model. There are many ways that such an evaluation can be done,[25] but a critical step is to 'play' with the model, to become familiar with its performance and to gain insights into the reasons for its behaviour. Does the model fit with prior expectations? If not, why not? Bear in mind that when model predictions are counter-intuitive, it may be that the model is satisfactory, but that the preconceptions are wrong. Thus when model outputs do not match expectations, it is timely to re-examine both our preconceptions and our data. Do our preconceptions (and the way we have collated these preconceptions into a mental model) fit with our understanding and our observations? Is it necessary to revise the model formulation (the grey model in Chapter 4)?

It may be that the preconception is right and the model is wrong, or that the data upon which the model was calibrated were inadequate. Flaws in the calibration data are all too common when data are based on surveys and observations rather than designed experiments (hence the desire to triangulate observations when calibrating the RiverMaker). It is possible for naïve interpretation of survey data to be completely misleading. A classic example of this was an investigation[26] into the effects of manuring on crop yields that showed that manure depressed crop yields. Anyone who has a garden and has grown vegetables knows that this is counter-intuitive. Further research revealed that farmers with manure were primarily interested in raising livestock, not in growing crops, and that those with the highest yields were vegetable growers who had no farmyard manure. This underscores the importance of careful interpretation of data from surveys and from opportunistic observations. To what extent have our preconceptions influenced our decisions about what data to collect and how to collect them?

One specific question that model builders should address at this stage is whether the model is complete in the sense that it is sufficient to deal with the questions being entertained. More specifically, whether any feedback loops have been omitted (for example, pests in crops; predators of stock; restrictions on people's activities). If so, to what extent would such oversights or simplifications affect the behaviour of the model?

In discussions leading to the RiverMaker model, we

canvassed a wide range of issues including opposition to the johads by authorities, about the need for maintenance of the earth walls, and the consequences of any adjacent villages having a 'free ride' – should they have been part of the model? We felt that these aspects could safely be omitted because they did not impinge greatly upon the main aspects of interest: the benefits realized by a village from johads and the consequences for downstream river flow. It is important to consider such questions, but it is equally important to confine a model to the essential features. It is easy to make a model complicated; the challenge is to make it simple while retaining the essential features and behaviour.

In the BroomGrass model, villagers wanted to include more detail about transport into the model because it was considered important ('Who provides transport, when and how much does it cost?'). These aspects were not included for logistical reasons associated with project management. Under different circumstances, they could have been included and may have offered deeper insights, but this does not mean the model was misleading or the process was useless. On the contrary, the modelling process helped the villagers to gain new insights and gave them the confidence to develop a better system for broomgrass harvesting.

Building confidence

Three aspects are involved in building user confidence in a model. Firstly, the model-building team must first build their own confidence in the model; the domain of acceptable performance should be defined; and finally, confidence should be established amongst key user groups. Let us consider these in turn.

Gaining self-confidence

Confidence in a model can be gained in many ways. An understanding of the model, a sense of ownership, and the ability to identify with some of the model outputs all contribute to this confidence. One effective way to foster confidence is to 'play' with a model in a structured way to better establish how it behaves under diverse circumstances, to locate any anomalies or errors, and to reinforce the ability to use it effectively. All members of the modelling team should learn how to use the model and try to understand how it works. They should understand where their intellectual property lies and should be comfortable that it has been correctly represented. They need to feel a sense of ownership and a sense of pride in the product.

When the broomgrass harvesters saw the first model outputs, they laughed. 'This is not right …' they said, and plunged on with the task of finding out why. A few hours later, they were happy with the model's behaviour. To a professional modeller, the resulting BroomGrass model was still naïve, but for the broomgrass harvesters, it was sufficient. They understood it and had gained new insights. They had sufficient confidence to change the communal rules for broomgrass harvesting and had no further need for the model.

Knowing the domain of utility

It is important that users are made aware of the range of starting conditions in which the model behaves reasonably, and that they are aware of any thresholds at which the model begins to look doubtful. In many ways, it does not matter if the model behaves badly at some extremes, as long as the thresholds defining the areas of doubtful reliability can be established and brought to the attention of users. Users can then be made aware of the domain within which the model gives trustworthy results, and of the circumstances under which model outputs should be regarded with scepticism.

This is something we do routinely in our daily lives, and with respected laws of physics. For instance, during a power failure, we might walk to the next room in the dark, but would probably find a torch or candle before going up or downstairs, a reflection of the trust we have in the mental model of our house. Similarly, we routinely use Newton's laws of motion, even though Einstein showed them to be inadequate. We have learned that Newton's laws are perfectly adequate for use on Earth, and are much easier to use than Einstein's alternative. Clearly, within the domain of utility, we settle for the simplest option.

With the RiverMaker model, we have come to trust the predictions about the number of days we can expect to find water in the wells and in the rivers, but we know that it would be unwise to attempt to predict crop yields or river volumes on the basis of predictions from this model. Similarly, the broomgrass ladies trusted the insights they had gained about grass ecology and scope for increased value adding, but knew that they should not make inferences about the timing or cost of transport to markets.

Communicating confidence

Some models, like the BroomGrass model, are designed only for personal use. Other models like the RiverMaker model are intended to help others gain new insights, while still others (for example, ZimFlores) are designed for others to use. If others are going to use a model, it is important to give them the confidence and enthusiasm to benefit from your own experience with the model, and empower them to build their own confidence. A large part of this is simply being able to explain and demonstrate the model. This does not mean that modellers should exaggerate a model's capabilities; on the contrary, it is often better to 'under-sell', and allow users to discover things for themselves. Most people like to try things, and they learn by doing, so an introduction to a model need not explain everything, but it should demonstrate enough to get them started and to give them confidence and enthusiasm.

This is not hard to achieve. Just two days after he was first introduced to modelling, Liswe Sibanda from Batanai had the enthusiasm to get up and explain his model with clarity and confidence to a modellers' seminar in Harare. There is no magical formula to achieve success like that with Liswe, but tools like The Power to Change game[27] can help to instil confidence and understanding.

Moving on

Once our model has been calibrated, and we are reasonably confident of its performance, it is time to move on to examine what we can learn from the model, exploring scenarios in a structured way to examine options and alternatives. It is important to follow through with this. Calibrating, testing and preparing a model for use is not easy, but it is important to reach this stage to reap the benefits and continue to strive towards our vision.

Notes

1   E. Muybridge (1878) 'Gaits of the Horse', Lantern slides from photographs made for Leland Stanford, Palo Alto, California, http://americanhistory.si.edu/muybridge/htm/htm_sec1/sec1.htm

2   'The River Maker', *New Scientist*, 7 September 2002, pp48–51.

3   Pani Yatra, Centre for Science and Environment Water Harvesting Campaign; see www.rainwaterharvesting.org/methods/paniyatra.htm.

4   R. Muetzelfeldt and J. Massheder (2003) 'The Simile visual modelling environment', *European Journal of Agronomy*, vol 18, pp345–358; J. K. Vanclay (2003) 'The one-minute modeller: An introduction to Simile', *Annals of Tropical Research*, vol 25, pp31–44; and other resources on the *Realizing Community Futures* website and CD (see page 143 for how to access these).

5   The equation is

        $d=s+ut+\frac{1}{2}at^2$

        where s is initial displacement, u is initial velocity, a is
        acceleration due to gravity and t is time.

6   This is easily done; see resources mentioned in Note 4
        above.

7   Based on rainfall data from International Water
        Management Institute and Rajasthan Department of
        Irrigation.

8   A. Sharma (2002) 'Does water harvesting help in
        water-scarce regions?', paper to Annual Partner's
        Meet, IWMI-Tata Water Policy Research Programme,
        International Water Management Institute.

9   The Central Groundwater Board of India uses three
        categories based on groundwater use as a percentage of
        annual recharge: white areas where use is less than 65
        per cent of recharge; light grey areas with 65–85 per
        cent of recharge; and darker areas where more than 85
        per cent of recharge is used. See Shah and Vengama
        Raju (2000).

10   See, for example, the resources mentioned in Notes 2
        and 3 above.

11   Ministry of Water Resources, India. See http://wrmin.
        nic.in/resource/physiographic.htm

12   *New Scientist*, 7 September 2002.

13   R. Mahapatra (1999) 'Waters of life', *Down to Earth*,
        15 March 1999, p38.

14   Z. Goldsmith (1998) 'Back to the future in
        Rajasthan', *The Ecologist*, vol 28, p222, July–August.

15   The groundwater table can rise 2–3 metres within
        15 days of the start of the monsoon, and had risen
        6 metres in some villages; recharge has raised the

groundwater from 200 to 20 feet below the surface; johads are filled to capacity by the end of the monsoon; before the johads were constructed, the river ran only for a few days each year during the monsoon; ten years after the construction of the first johad, the river began to flow again. R. K. Srinivasan and Suresh Babu (2001) 'People fight back', *CatchWater*, vol 3, no 4, pp1–3; Shree Padre (2000) 'Harvesting the monsoon: Livelihoods reborn', *ILEIA Newsletter*, March 2000, pp14–15; A. Sharma in Note 8; R. Mahapatra in Note 11; Z. Goldsmith in Note 12.

16   M. Haggith and R. Prabhu (2003) 'Unlocking complexity: The importance of idealization in simulation modelling', *Small-scale Forest Economics, Management and Policy*, vol 2, pp293–312.

17   Over 360 per cent per year according to the UN Office for the Coordination of Humanitarian Affairs, IRIN News, 17 July 2003, www.irinnews.org/report.asp?ReportID=35466

18   E. Wenger (1998) *Communities of Practices: Learning, Meaning and Identity*, Cambridge University Press, Cambridge.

19   D. A. Kolb (1986) *Experiential Learning: Experience as the Source of Learning and Development,* Prentice-Hall, Englewood Cliffs, NJ.

20   We have attempted to achieve 20 iterations over 10 days.

21   M. Haggith, R. I. Muetzelfeldt and J. Taylor (2003) 'Modelling decision-making in rural communities at the forest margin', *Small-scale Forest Economics, Management and Policy*. vol 2, pp241–258.

22   Some 233 parameters, plus 905 records of land ownership and area from a GIS, and 1057 rainfall observations from the Bureau of Meteorology.

23   http://nssdc.gsfc.nasa.gov/database/MasterCatalog?sc=1998-073A

24   'NASA identifies "likely direct cause" of Genesis crash', *Scientific American*, 18 October 2004, available at www.sciam.com/article.cfm?articleID=000BBC43-3ED5-1170-BED583414B7F0000.

25   J. K. Vanclay and J. P. Skovsgaard (1997) 'Evaluating forest growth models', *Ecological Modelling*, vol 98, pp1–12.

26   G. W. Snedecor and W. G. Cochran (1980) *Statistical Methods*, 7th edn, Iowa University Press.

27   Available on the *Realizing Community Futures* website and CD (see page 143 for how to access these).

6 Exploring alternatives

Two roads diverged in a yellow wood,
And sorry I could not travel both
And be one traveler, long I stood
And looked down one as far as I could
To where it bent in the undergrowth;

Then took the other, as just as fair,
And having perhaps the better claim,
Because it was grassy and wanted wear …

… And that has made all the difference.

Robert Frost, *The Road Not Taken*[1]

Modelling empowers us to 'look further down alternative roads' and make an informed choice from the options available to us. Unlike Robert Frost's traveller, who could see only as far as the next bend and who chose his path 'because it was grassy and wanted wear', we can use models in various ways to evaluate our options and consider the implications. For instance, we could use a map to see where the two roads might lead us. A map is completely descriptive and does not help us to divine the future, but it does help us orient ourselves in unfamiliar situations and make an informed choice from the options available. Predicting what might happen in the future if we make alternative choices today is more difficult, but still worthwhile. Most people plan for their old age: villagers in India may plan their family and arrange their children's marriages to try to improve their future prospects, while the urban middle class, in Mumbai and New York alike, seek investment advice to ascertain the financial viability of their retirement plans. Investment advisers cannot be sure what will happen in the future, but they can devise a scenario based on 'business as usual' assumptions to indicate if our current plan is likely to provide for our future needs. Such a simplistic outline of a possible future may be an important step in appreciating whether there is a problem and whether new initiatives are needed, both in our personal lives, and with broader social and natural resource issues.

The weather report offers another familiar example. Many people regularly take note of the weather forecast, even though they are sceptical about its accuracy and still get caught in unexpected rainstorms from time to time. Despite these surprises, we still find the weather report useful to consider our options. When the weather follows a familiar pattern, we may have little need for a forecast, but when we enter unfamiliar territory, perhaps when we travel to a new destination, or when we unexpectedly experience a severe storm, we turn to the weather report with renewed interest to learn what may unfold and to discover why things are different.

Computer-based models allow us to 'look ahead' into simulated futures, allowing us to play out scenarios that might happen and to consider our options in many fields of endeavour. They allow us to see how we might realize our vision and to understand possible implications. Close to the truth, yet far from it, these scenarios spark ideas, innovation and learning. So we move finally in this chapter to explore how our visions might play out in the future and to consider what actions may be required for them to be realized. Welcome to the future!

Alternatives and outcomes

As we have just discussed, most people are routinely faced with choices in which they need to make a decision with consequences that are not fully apparent. In ZimFlores, a farmer needs to plant maize for subsistence. The decision about when to plant is influenced by season, soil moisture, available labour and other factors. In other situations, a farmer might rely on a weather forecast to help him decide if the outlook is sufficiently promising to start planting.

Weather forecasts come in many forms. We are all familiar with the daily weather report ('Tomorrow will be 32°C and sunny'), but there are also specialized forecasts made for particular consumers. Farmers may rely on a ten-day weather forecast, which estimates the probability that the cumulative ten-day rainfall exceeds some threshold. Airlines rely on much shorter, more specific forecasts ('Our flight has been delayed because the fog at our destination is not expected to clear until 9.00am'). The resources used to prepare these forecasts are the same, but the products differ according to the need.

Meteorologists no longer simply provide a forecast. Most forecasts are accompanied by their rationale, usually in the form of a weather map and a satellite image showing how the weather is expected to develop during the period of the forecast. These supporting materials help to educate consumers about how the weather behaves, by helping them to become familiar with weather patterns and to understand how the speed at which a front (or depression) approaches may affect the forecast conditions. And so it is with modelling the interactions between people and natural resources. To be relevant, simulations must be customized to the problem at hand and to the needs of the stakeholder. In addition, simulation outputs form just a small part of the process, which may be ineffective without participation and understanding.

RiverMaker

As we have seen in Chapter 3, johads have helped revive communities and rivers in Alwar district. To some, Rajendra Singh and the TBS[2] are heroes and the johads are a success story, whereas to others, they posed a threat. Warrants were issued for the removal of their first johad under the Irrigation and Drainage Act, and Rajendra was assaulted by an official in Uttar Pradesh. Scientists at the International Water Management Institute (IWMI) argued that 'There is thus a need for a scientific examination of the hydrological credentials of river basins before embarking on programs to establish water-harvesting systems. ... The debates and issues are all too real to be ignored ...'.[3] One of IWMI's concerns was that johads would impact on water users downstream, and they apparently chose not to rely on various reports about rivers 'coming to life' with perennial flow. The RiverMaker model could have been useful to Rajendra Singh in helping to defuse opposition to his proposals by authorities, and could provide a basis to resolve IWMI's concerns. Simulations show that cumulative river flow over several years is not greatly affected by johads. Without the johads, water rushes off the hills in a series of flash floods. With the johads, the flood peaks are reduced and the dry-season base flow is increased, with the result that over a period of several years, the anticipated cumulative river flow does not change much after johads are built (see Figure 6.1). In this case, two key scenarios centre on downstream river flow with and without

Figure 6.1 Simulation of catchments with (lower line) and without (upper line) johads, showing the impact on cumulative river flow (gigalitres) and the moderating effect of johads in slowing runoff and maintaining baseflow during the dry season (inset)

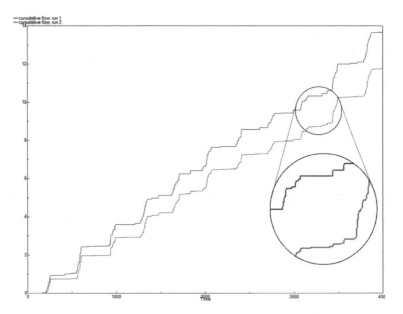

johads. Such a comparison relies on simulation and cannot be done in real life, because no two river basins and no two monsoons are the same, so paired experiments are not possible.

While Figure 6.1 is informative, it is unlikely, on its own, to influence IWMI scientists who had already chosen to disregard reports about rivers 'coming to life'. The model that produced the figure is likely to be much more effective in influencing opinion because users can experience it for themselves. IWMI scientists would find it easy to understand the model and could run it for themselves and watch the scenarios unfold. They could adjust the model to be consistent with their own experience and explore the implications arising from different viewpoints about river dynamics and johad design. The provision of a model introduces the possibility to explore the middle ground. Researchers could not only explore the two scenarios with and without the TBS johads, but could also use the model to investigate the consequences of limiting johads to a specified size, or of drawing on IWMI's expertise in locating the johads in the landscape.

Despite the Ramon Magsaysay prize and evidence of rivers 'coming to life', the construction of traditional water-harvesting structures remains contentious. The Rajasthan Irrigation Department prevented repairs to the Lava Ka Baas dam and took the matter to the High Court in Rajasthan.[4] The issue is also topical elsewhere in India, as state governments in Madhya Pradesh and Karnataka are embarking on large watershed programmes with a strong emphasis on traditional water-harvesting structures.

BroomGrass

The BroomGrass model was developed because of concerns that traditional harvesting practices were not sustainable. CIFOR's Adaptive Co-Management programme brought together villagers dependent on the broomgrass resource and helped them to explore their options and propose a plan for action. This process revealed many complex issues surrounding the broomgrass resource, the answers to which were elusive. Participatory modelling formed the basis for social learning and provided the knowledge and insights that fed back into the reflection, learning and action cycle. While the model they developed was unsophisticated, the whole process was useful in helping people explore scenarios. Their scenarios included 'business as usual' (continuing to dig the grass), using peer pressure to switch to grass cutting and outlawing uprooting, trying to influence transport prices, and several options for adding value to their product and increasing market share by making their brooms more attractive to customers. While many of these scenarios proved fanciful when discussed at greater length, the process of generating alternatives based on analysis of their model was successful in empowering people to explore options, and then to run with their best bet, even before getting to the stage of running computer simulations of their various options.

Figure 6.2 Simulation run with the BroomGrass model showing grass biomass
(top graph) and household wealth (bottom graph) for business as usual
(lower line) and under the new initiatives (upper line), simulated for
50 months (4 years)

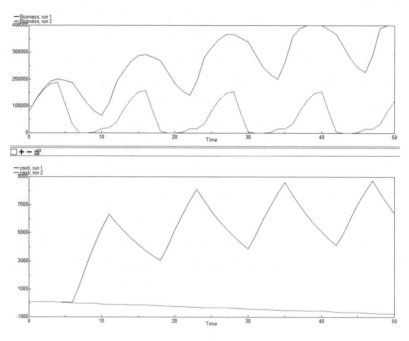

Figure 6.2 illustrates two of the scenarios considered:
business as usual and the scenario that was finally adopted (peer pressure,
adding value and so on). It is evident that business as usual is a downward
spiral, with households caught in a poverty trap and the broomgrass resource
gradually being depleted. The new initiatives proposed by the villagers
lead to an improvement in household wealth and allow the broomgrass
resource to recover. While Figure 6.2 shows the magnitude of the changes
anticipated, it is somewhat sterile and does not reveal the social interaction,
the learning or the new-found confidence. Figure 6.3 may be more revealing
in this regard, with the Gababe broomgrass collectors showing off their new
clothes and their decorated brooms made from cut grass.

Figure 6.3 Gababe broomgrass collectors with their new brooms
Source: Ravi Prabhu

ZimFlores

ZimFlores was oriented more towards evaluating broader policy options. Some people perceived that the key issue for resource sustainability in the Mafungautsi region of Zimbabwe was saving the forest, and that the way to do this was to provide more forest officers to patrol the forest. Others felt that the forest was not directly under threat, that additional forest officers could do little to change harvesting patterns, and that local social

Figure 6.4 Simulation showing the expected impact of extra patrols
by forest officers

Note: Graphs show average number of poles in each of the three forest areas (per hectare, top left),
basal area (m²/ha, top right), poles harvested by each of the three villages (poles/year, bottom left)
and average wealth of households ('dosh', bottom right). Each graph shows six lines corresponding
to the two scenarios (status quo; increased patrols) and three forest areas (top) or villages (bottom).

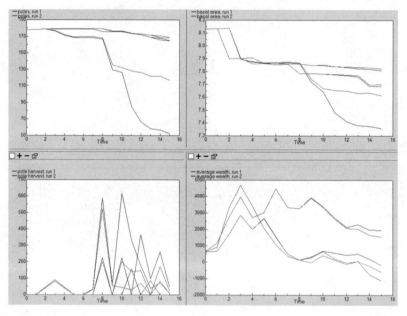

institutions held the key issue to sustainable resource use. ZimFlores helped
people to explore these issues in a structured way. The ZimFlores approach
to simulation modelling differs from classical system dynamics in that the
latter focuses on a single *problem*,[5] whereas the former recognizes that there
may be many spatially and temporally related issues that are chronic rather
than acute.

ZimFlores simulations demonstrate that additional patrols
by forest officers may help to reduce harvesting of poles (compare lower pair
of lines in Figure 6.4 top left) and maintain the stand basal area (top right),
but only if patrols are sufficiently frequent to disrupt 20 per cent of these
attempts. A lower frequency of patrols (for example, disrupting 15 per cent
of attempts) was ineffective and contributed a negligible reduction in pole

harvesting. ZimFlores is not sufficiently accurate to be precise about this 20 per cent threshold, but the discovery of this previously unimagined threshold stimulates discussion about the efficacy and timing of patrols by forest officers.

ZimFlores encourages the exploration of alternative initiatives to reduce illicit forest harvesting. One alternative that was evaluated was inspired by the BroomGrass model. This alternative (illustrated in Figure 6.5) simulates peer pressure for more equitable sharing of common property resources and greater value adding to the brooms. This alternative is more effective in reducing illicit harvesting of poles and contributes to greater household wealth (in contrast to increased patrols, which reduce household wealth – see Figure 6.4).

Figure 6.5 Simulation of broomgrass reforms, with more equitable sharing of common resources and greater value adding to brooms

Note: Graphs show average number of poles/ha in each forest (top left), total thatch harvest (per year, top right), average household income from thatch (dosh/year, bottom left), and household wealth (dosh, bottom right). Run 1 reflects the same scenario as presented in Figure 6.4.

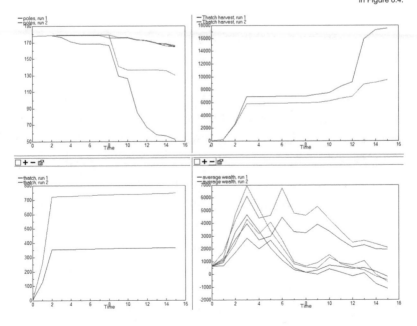

Models like ZimFlores encourage stakeholders to consider alternative ways to find win–win outcomes, and provide an objective way to appraise these alternatives, to stimulate discussion of these alternatives, and to move the discussion towards a resolution. These alternatives that stakeholders may propose give rise to a series of scenarios, each reflecting the outcome expected under a given course of action. These scenarios may canvass a wide range of possibilities, but should be related to the problem at hand to enable stakeholders to see if the problem is 'solved', is circumvented or is unavoidable. Since there may be more than one 'solution' to a problem, a wide range of scenarios should be simulated. The set of scenarios under consideration can usefully include the supposition that the problem has been overcome, with the model being used to examine how that desired outcome might have been reached. In many cases, key focal issues relate to livelihoods (for example, basic income and food security) and resource sustainability indicators (for example, forest area, relative densities of trees and other useful forest plants), and these should be canvassed in the development of scenarios for evaluation.

Trying new things, recognizing success, comparing outcomes

We can measure the width or wear of a road, but our decision about which road to take may be much more subjective. The height of a person is judged by a standard yardstick, but beauty is in the eye of the beholder. Clearly, we have well-defined criteria to choose the tallest in a group, but choosing the most beautiful is more problematic. In gauging the 'best' outcome from a series of simulations, we need to establish explicit criteria. It is not simply a question of recognizing utopia when we reach it, because 'knowing how way leads on to way', we often search for a direction of travel rather than a destination. There are many ways that alternative scenarios can be contrasted, and the benefits of modelling are best realized when explicit criteria for comparison are established and agreed upon.

With the RiverMaker, useful discussions with IWMI scientists cannot be based only upon projected data on river flow (Figure 6.1), because that overlooks the purpose of the johads. Rajendra Singh and the villagers built the johads to make water available to villages in the dark zone; water for drinking and cooking, for stock and for irrigation. So any discussion about an appropriate compromise should illustrate not only the downstream river flow, but also the availability of sufficient water in the dark zone villages. Modelling environments such as Simile make it easy to graph data, but the challenge is to devise diagnostic indicators. In RiverMaker, variables such as annual percentage of days with water in wells or the depth to water in wells could be enlightening (for example, Figure 6.6), but it is preferable to let participants devise their own indicators that sum up what is important to them, and what will be useful in judging the

Figure 6.6 Some useful indicators of the effect of johads include the percentage of days with water in wells (top) and depth of water in wells (bottom)

Note: Without johads, the simulation is always zero; the visible lines reflect a simulation of the situation after construction of johads.

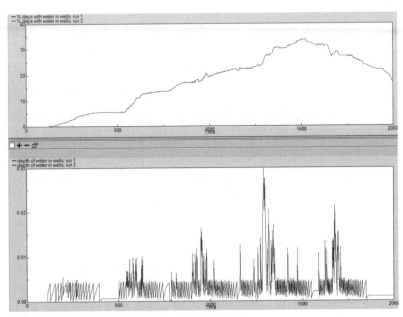

viability of alternative courses of action. The role of the modeller in this process is to help participants express their ideas as explicit constructs that can be represented in (and graphed by) the model. Modellers may also assist by drawing the attention of participants to some of the specialist display tools available in Simile (for example, to map landscapes, create dynamic diagrams of forests and fish, and illustrate stream flow).

Focus on the solution

In Chapter 5 we introduced a diagram of the modelling cycle and explored the need to focus, idealize and simplify. This need continues during the process of model testing, where it is important to adapt a systematic approach to calibrating and testing a model. A set of scenarios that can stimulate and direct group discussions towards an effective solution do not arise through random 'fiddles' with diverse aspects of a model. Instead, we should follow an approach akin to that used in calibrating RiverMaker in Chapter 5, starting with a key suggestion or possible solution that might well work, fine-tuning it to get it 'right', and progressing to systematically vary key elements of this baseline, to demonstrate its strengths and weaknesses. In short, to focus on the solution, idealize key components contributing to this solution, and simplifying the simulation to reveal why these are key elements in a solution, and how they influence the outcome.

Many modelling textbooks recommend a problem-based approach. This is good advice when there is a simple problem (for example, modelling the trajectory of a stone), but is rarely a tractable approach when the problems are many, complex and chronic. In such cases, it is more useful to adopt a vision-oriented approach (as was done by the broomgrass harvesters, who wanted to pursue their ideas about value adding and peer pressure) or an issue-oriented approach (as we have seen done with River-Maker and the issue of well water in the dark zone).

Either way, we progress by developing and iteratively improving an understanding of the key drivers, even though they may not always be obvious. Our hope is that we can learn this while model building, and that modelling will offer new insights and viewpoints. If the model is built systematically around processes that are understood and can be calibrated, it may reveal insights not previously suspected (such as the threshold for forest patrols). A model may even reveal that the 'usual suspects' may be less important than was initially assumed. However, such discoveries may depend on a systematic approach to model building; models that rely on an observed correlation between the 'usual suspect' and the output of interest will not reveal counter-intuitive insights. A model that appears to suggest some surprises warrants further work, as these surprises could arise because our premonition is wrong, or because our model is wrong. Thus surprising results indicate a need to experiment with the model to develop a better understanding and to modify the model until it behaves as expected, or until our expectations change.

'Best bet' and other strategies

Key stakeholders often have an idea of the 'best bet' in many situations, but may not have the confidence to articulate it fully, or may not have thought through all the details. Models can assist stakeholders by providing a structured way to explore the elements and implications of a 'best bet', both through the process of thinking about and constructing the model, and by using the model to see what might happen under different circumstances.

The 'best bet' for the broomgrass resource, to cut rather than dig the grass, originated among the people who rely on the resource. Foreign experts claimed it made no difference, so the community did their own experiment to convince themselves that their best bet was in fact, the best option. Modelling gave them further confidence in their best bet and helped them place their best bet in a broader context because it provided the stimulus to think through the problem in a structured way. Cutting the grass is just part of a broader strategy, which also includes peer group pressure (the carrot and stick approach), and decorating the brooms to add value and secure market share. The BroomGrass model succeeded because it did what the participants needed and did not offer things that they could not understand. The secret to its success is that the villagers built the model themselves, consistent with their own view of the world, and in doing so, gained the confidence needed to establish a new paradigm for broomgrass harvesting, broom making and marketing.

The broomgrass stakeholders did not need to carry out extensive simulations with their model; the process of thinking through the problem in a structured way was sufficient to give them the insights and confidence needed to achieve a new paradigm. This is not always the case. In the case of the Mafungautsi forest, stakeholders were divided over the ability of patrols to curb illicit tree removal, but neither supporters nor sceptics of patrols suspected the existence of a threshold, below which patrols were ineffective. Many stakeholders felt that patrols would be ineffective and that the solution to sustainable forest utilization lay in adding value to other activities. The ZimFlores model offered an objective way for these and other issues to be explored and resolved. Whilst ZimFlores has proved useful, its possibilities have not yet been exhausted, and it may be used to explore emerging issues not yet canvassed, in an effort to find new solutions for new circumstances and challenges.

In the 'real world', it is rare for there to be a single solution to a resource-use problem. Most resource conflicts involve complex issues that may have many 'solutions' and involve challenges that require adaptive responses from stakeholders. Dealing with such issues is never easy, and participatory modelling offers a structured process to develop greater insights and allow objective analysis of alternatives.

Evaluate scenarios

In situations involving resource-use conflicts, good solutions are rarely obvious, and it may not be easy to find a workable solution among several candidate simulations. We have emphasized that careful thought and consultation are needed to construct useful models and to devise insightful scenarios. The same care, thought and consultation are needed when evaluating scenarios to find mutually satisfactory outcomes. Central to this process is the need to find diagnostic criteria that can shed light on the issues raised by stakeholders. Stakeholders should consider how they would recognize a good solution and how they would *know* that it was a good outcome, both for themselves and for their fellow stakeholders. Such criteria need not take the form of a single index; stakeholders may find that other model outputs (perhaps in the form of graphs or maps) may be better at revealing the comparative advantage of each option under consideration.

In making a decision, people are influenced both by quantitative and qualitative data. Stakeholders evaluating scenarios are no exception and should be encouraged to articulate both quantitative and qualitative objectives. The challenge for the modeller and facilitator is to help formulate diagnostic displays that best reveal the comparative advantage of each option under consideration.

Broomgrass modellers included the 'beauty' of the brooms as a variable. To accomplished modellers, this may seem a naïve expression, but for the people in question it served as a useful indicator to signal their intention to attempt additional value adding. It reflected their first consideration of decoration of brooms as a way to overcome market resistance to brooms made from cut (rather than dug) grass, to command a higher price, and to gain market share.

Another example is the use by both Kenyan and Nepali farmers of 'appetite satisfaction' in cattle.[6] This is generally ignored even in participatory research because many scientists are uncomfortable with it, but it is a key to understanding farmers' decisions on diet selection. When fodder is scarce, farmers want to satisfy appetite for as long as possible with minimum feed, in order to control animal behaviour (important when animals are tethered close to the house), and so they value low digestibility feeds that are conventionally seen by fodder scientists as of low value.

Many readers, like the IWMI scientists, may have been initially sceptical of the ability of a few johads to alleviate the water shortage within the dark zone, but a few simulations quickly demonstrate their effect. In this way, simulations can be an important part of the brainstorm-and-reflect cycle. 'Public' brainstorming can be embarrassing, unless well facilitated, and people may be reluctant to offer their wildest ideas. This is where modelling may help expand the pool of ideas, as it allows private 'brainstorming' with seemingly wild ideas screened before they are offered up for wider discussion.

Learning through simulation

Participatory modelling is not just a good way to find 'solutions' to challenging problems, but also an effective way to engage communities in facilitated discussion and experiential learning. It can provide a gentle introduction into the use of evidence-based reasoning that can lead on to action research. It encourages participants to engage in the modelling cycle of puzzle, hypothesize, test and reflect (see Figure 5.7). This cycle leads people to reflect on the relevance of proposed interventions and thus to learn about the system under study.

Sometimes it is the process of thinking about a model, not the simulation output or the model itself, that is the key 'product' of a modelling exercise. For instance, with the broomgrass collectors, modelling offered a new way of presenting ideas, a way that was not previously available to the Gababe community. Efforts by the stakeholders to model the broomgrass system provided a focus to their discussion, a new dimension to their thinking, and a basis for evaluating alternatives. The resulting model has little utility for others (other than as a case study), but it has served its purpose in facilitating reform and fostering sustainable use of the resource.

Gaining confidence

To achieve the outcomes that we have illustrated, stakeholders must have confidence in the model. In many resource conflicts, stakeholders are suspicious of experts affiliated with official land management agencies and may suspect a hidden agenda. Participatory modelling fosters understanding and builds trust and a sense of ownership by all stakeholders in the model and the process. This ownership, trust and understanding are critical to finding a solution in situations where there is strong dissent among stakeholders, and can be fostered through a few simple steps:

- start with a simple model, easily accessible to participants (perhaps a diagram in the sand);
- gradually expand the scope of the model, with the introduction of additional features and feedbacks led by stakeholder discussions;
- help participants to understand model notation, so that they retain an overview – and ownership – of the model, even though they may not fully comprehend all the nuances;
- demonstrate the use of the model and present simulation outputs, not only of 'typical' situations, but also of extreme scenarios, 'impossible dreams', and unexpected outcomes (it is often the surprises that offer the greatest insights);
- make sure the model is always accessible for the participants to examine their suspicions and scenarios (both by giving away copies of the model, and by providing access to a trusted modeller to act as their agent).

As national sports teams are aware, friendly competition can be a good way
to defuse hostilities and foster productive friendships. Thus well-facilitated
role plays can contribute to a shared understanding and help pave the way
towards solutions in resource conflicts. In the same way, competition with
simulation models can be constructive and insightful. To this end, CIFOR
has developed The Power to Act, an interface suited to many resource situations that enables competitive play with simulation models to explore long-
term consequences in a common property context.[7] We encourage you to
experiment with this package to gain confidence in the ability of simulation
models to offer such insights.

Consolidating experience

For stakeholders to learn through simulation, their experience with models
needs to be consolidated and should challenge their preconceptions. Stakeholders should not be 'bystanders'. It is not sufficient for them to observe a
simulation and think 'that's odd' or 'that's interesting'; effective facilitators
should ensure that they reflect on these observations, consider the implications, and continue with the modelling cycle of puzzle, hypothesize, test,
reflect (Figure 5.7). Timely group discussions and field trips underpinned
by simulation studies can be effective ways to help stubborn stakeholders
to develop their understanding and move towards a shared solution. Such
reality checks should focus on any perceived inconsistencies, should try to
identify the critical elements of potential solutions, and should attempt
to appraise the risks (for example, 'What will happen if we do nothing?';
'What if our understanding of the feedback loops is wrong?'). These questions can be hard to resolve in discussion and in real life, but can – and
should – be evaluated with simulation models.

Understanding implications

Perhaps the most important implication of models is the opportunity for
us to do 'low cost' experiments, experiments that we cannot risk in real life,

and to learn from errors that are of no consequence. The airline industry makes extensive use of flight simulators to train pilots, investigate accidents, and to help maintain safety in the industry. When there is an accident or a near-miss involving pilot error, all pilots flying similar aircraft are required to gain experience with that scenario in a flight simulator, to help reduce the risk of another incident. Crashes in the simulator are an acceptable part of learning, but crashes in real life must be avoided because they are expensive in terms of human life, equipment and the environment. So it is with natural resources. Bad management decisions can be disastrous for people, their livelihoods and for the environment. We should use models, which we share and trust, to evaluate our decisions in a simulation environment in which disasters do not matter. Having explored the options of interest, we can then pursue our best strategy secure in the knowledge that we have taken 'due diligence' in ensuring the best outcome for all concerned.

Would you fly with a pilot who had not completed the flight simulator training? Would you take natural resource decisions without the same degree of diligence?

Notes

1   R. Frost (1915) 'The Road Not Taken', first published in *Atlantic Monthly*, August 1915, but widely available in poetry anthologies and editions of Frost's poems, such as *Collected Poems, Prose, and Plays* (Library of America, 1995).

2   Tarun Bhagat Sangh or Young India Association.

3   A. Sharma (2002) 'Does water harvesting help in water-scarce regions?' paper to Annual Partners' Meet, IWMI-Tata Water Policy Research Program, International Water Management Institute, p23.

4   Sunny Sebastian (2003) 'Villagers' efforts washed away', *The Hindu*, 16 July.

5   See for example, J. Ashby, C. Bergmark, F. J. C.
     Chandler, W. D. Dar, A. El-Beltagy, W. Erskine,
     L. Harrington, R. R. Harwood, D. Keatinge,
     P. A. Sanchez, M. Swift and B. Walker (2000)
     *Integrated Natural Resource Management Research in
     the CGIAR*, www.inrm.cgiar.org/Workshop2000/
     Meeting%20Result/result.htm.

6   B. Thapa, D. H. Walker and F. L. Sinclair (1997)
     'Indigenous knowledge of the feeding value of tree
     fodder', *Animal Feed Science and Technology*, vol 67,
     pp97–114.

7   A copy is available on the *Realizing Community
     Futures* website and CD (see page 143 for how to
     access these).

Into the future

Que será, será
Whatever will be, will be
The future's not ours to see …

Ray Evans and Jay Livingston,
'Que será, será'[1]

'What will be, will be', the old song reminds us, lest our new-found enthusiasm misleads us into believing that we now have the powers of an oracle! The future is truly not ours to see, but it has been ours to play with. Like good chess players we've studied a lot of possible moves and with the quiet confidence of a player who is well prepared, we are now ready to make our move. And yet we know that surprises are inevitable and the future is still going to be a big adventure! It is time now to take a last look around, consolidate what we know, gather up what we need, and step out into a future that is now less daunting.

A last look back

Our journey so far has taken us through very different and probably unfamiliar territory. We have moved fast, skipping steps and jumping hurdles in the process. It is perhaps time now to reflect a little on our journey in order to consolidate what we have learnt.

In the past, the use of computer models and simulation has been perceived by many people to be mainly about foretelling the future. Thus we have seen big models like World3[2] that warned of Malthusian disaster, and models that tried to predict the rise and fall of the stock market. Not surprisingly, many of these predictions proved untrue. Although in each of these cases our understanding of relationships and systems may have improved, computer modelling and forecasting fell into disrepute. It did not help that most of these models were written in complex computer code understandable to very few people. Despite this heritage, computer models are still used widely on a daily basis for forecasting. Our daily weather report is a good example of such a forecast. Although weather forecasting has got a lot better in recent years, that proverbial pinch of salt remains necessary!

In this book we have not been very concerned with forecasting. Our interest has been to envision the future and then work out how best to get there. This is an approach that is called 'backcasting' in the literature.[3] Backcasting is being used increasingly to help work out possible courses of action in the face of an unknowable future. It is less controversial simply because it does not pretend to be an oracle. A good example of how backcasting is helping to determine future courses of action on a global scale is the Global Environmental Outlook.[4] Here experts have defined four scenarios (only one of them can be described as a vision in our sense) and have used computer simulations to work out what would happen to the environment and to people if those scenarios were realized. This is more akin to a chess player working through potential situations than to a wizard foretelling the future.

Much modelling today simply takes place because people want to clarify their own understanding about a complex issue. It has become a tool for bringing people's mental models of their world to the surface and allowing them to be reconciled with each other.[5] In this context, modelling is a form of communication, negotiation and conflict resolution. This role for modelling has become possible because of the advances in the tools and techniques for modelling. Throughout this book we have used a modelling technique called system dynamics, devised in the 1950s by Jay Forrester at the Massachusetts Institute of Technology.[6] It has become widely accessible only in the last decade or so with the advent of graphical user interfaces that make it possible to build models with diagrams instead of writing computer code. The beauty of these platforms[7] is that the diagram that forms the basis of the model is intuitively understandable to many people, and better still, the diagram works! System dynamics, as we have said, is only one approach to modelling. There are several others, but most of them tend not to have the kind of software support enjoyed by system dynamics approaches.

In Chapter 4, we illustrated how the system dynamics approach can be an expressive way for ordinary people to represent their understanding about their environment. Such a representation has two important benefits. It is explicit and rigorous, so that it helps express our understanding more clearly and fully, and in doing so, we often discover inconsistencies or gaps in our own understanding. In addition, it helps us share our understanding with others. We continued in Chapter 5 to illustrate how common phenomena and seemingly casual observations could be used to calibrate and test a model, especially when observations from diverse sources could be used to cross-check inferences. Some readers may doubt that such methods can contribute to a reliable model. We do not suggest that the approach we advocate should be used to establish whether an industrial plantation will yield a return on investment in excess of the interest rate on the loan; there are other well-established tools for such analyses. However, our approach may be useful to explore whether an industrial plantation is in the best interests of the local community and ecosystem. Donella Meadows[8] compiled a list of 12 'leverage points' that could be used to make changes for the better. Numbers, parameters and constants were right at the bottom of this list, whereas goals, rules of the system (incentives and peer pressure) and feedback loops were near the top of the list. We are not suggesting that correctly estimating the value of parameters is unimportant, but we are saying that the need to estimate these variables should not become an obstacle to realizing our visions. Einstein did not supersede Newton's laws by close scrutiny of the parameters in his equations; he looked at the big picture rather than the fine detail. Many of the scenarios examined in Chapter 6 reveal large differences in the indicators of interest; differences so large that fine adjustments to most variables will not change the ranking of scenarios.

In Chapter 6, we examined how to use these new-found tools to explore scenarios and see how our visions can be attained. The magnitude of the task should not be underestimated, but our experience is that ordinary people, when motivated and assisted, can complete models that are sophisticated, reliable and useful in developing new insights. And it is these insights, not the models, that form the important outcomes. We have seen that these insights can change, and have changed, the world for the better!

Gearing up for the future

It is our intention that when you put down this book you will better appreciate what goes into producing such scenarios, to be able to appraise how close – or far – from reality they are, or to be persuaded to use computer-based simulations to try and realize your visions. If you are new to modelling, you can do this by teaming up with people who already have skills and experience with computer models who can help you with turning your vision into a computer simulation. You may even wish to improve your own modelling skills as a result, or simply read more about the subject. In either case, resources are available to help you. In the Resources section we offer a list of some of the resources that we have found to be useful. Additionally there is information, links to internet resources, examples and modelling software on the website that supports this book, www.cifor.cgiar.org/RealizingFutures (or for those without internet connectivity, on the CD available on request)[9]. We have presented this information in an interactive easy-to-use manner, and hope that you will have fun exploring it!

Some sceptics may doubt the applicability of system dynamics approaches to social problems, or doubt the ability of ordinary people to deal with these issues. Such comments are usually made by people who have not experimented with system dynamics modelling. Jay Forrester turned his attention to social problems[10] after establishing the utility of system dynamics in industry. He clearly believed that the method was equally applicable to social situations. Our point of departure is that we advocate that people should build these models themselves, following their own vision, to explore implications and devise a strategy to find a way forward. Some may consider this a big 'ask' of rural people, but our case studies illustrate that this can be done. Here again, other people who have tried this are also convinced it can be done. For the last 25 years Nancy Roberts[11] has been active in using system dynamics to improve understanding in schools. Clearly, youth is no barrier, and it is our experience that the absence of formal schooling is also no barrier to effective problem solving through visioning and participatory modelling.

From scenarios to actions

We all know that the transition from a pleasant dream to reality is very often a rather unpleasant thump! There is always the danger that in the process of turning a vision into a computer simulation, exploring that simulation becomes an end in itself, an end in which a game is played for its own rewards, rather than as a means to deal with the future. This certainly appears to have happened with some modelling efforts in the past, but it is not our intention, and our case studies illustrate that good outcomes are possible.

Rajendra Singh did not have access to our approach, but has indicated in discussions with us that he believes that sharing his ideas through modelling, like our River-maker case study, could have eased traumatic negotiations with government officials. The broomgrass collectors of Batanai are clear evidence of the impacts that can be achieved. The grass on the *vlei* is more abundant and the people of Batanai village are better off, both financially and socially, having gained new confidence in their ability to shape their destiny. Benefits of the ZimFlores experience are more difficult to highlight, but it is clear that all those involved gained new insights into the dynamics of the socio-environmental system at Mafungautsi. There are no longer calls for more forest guards, and development workers are now working with local people to make better use of the broomgrass and thatchgrass and of other non-wood forest resources.

It is interesting to look at computer chess as an analogy to natural resource management. For many years, the chess masters have prepared carefully for matches, using records of past games and playing with their seconds. Since 1988, when the Deep Thought computer performed well in championships, and especially since 1997, when Deep Blue won a match against the grandmaster Gary Kasparov, chess masters have also used computer programmes and databases to assist in their preparation. But man versus computer matches have had a short life, not because computers have become too good,[12] but because computers play faultless but uninspiring chess. According to Kasparov, the future of chess is 'advanced chess',[13] in which a human player and a computer chess program collaborate and compete as a team against other such pairs. Kasparov's view is that this will increase the standard of play to levels never before seen, and will produce blunder-free games with both perfect tactical play and skilful strategy. The strength of an advanced chess player lies in this combination of the computer's tactical accuracy and the human's creativity and sagacity.[14] This is an important analogy for natural resource management: the vision and strategy must come from the people, while the strength of the model is to ensure that initiatives are thoroughly researched and free from errors. Advanced natural resource management will rely on collaboration between people and models, with stakeholders providing the vision, and the model assisting with quality assurance. As Albert Einstein once remarked: 'Computers are incredibly fast, accurate and stupid; humans are incredibly slow, inaccurate and brilliant; together they are powerful beyond imagination.'[15] We need to apply this power to natural resource management.

Final advice

The chapters of this book are laid out in a linear fashion: a common problem, a shared vision that progressively becomes explicit and substantive, and finally a model that can be used to explore implications. In real life, progress is rarely like that; we often need to retrace our steps. At every step of this process, it is quite usual to discover something, something that makes the group return to a previous step with deeper insights, clearer vision, and more information to contribute to the analysis. Thus rather than a neat linear process, progress is made in a spiral pattern, continually returning to earlier steps, but each time, dealing with these at a higher level. Participants should not be alarmed if they appear to be retracing their steps; they should be reassured that this is part of the learning process, and is usually a good sign of progress. However, it does mean that the process should not be rushed to meet a deadline, but should be allowed to mature at its own pace.

The approach we advocate is not a panacea. It is a useful tool, but it is just one tool in the toolbox of action research. In some cases, such as the three case studies that we have highlighted in this book, structured learning through participatory modelling may be the best way forward. But there will be other situations where other tools are more suitable. We have found our approach helpful, so urge you to become sufficiently familiar with it that you can recognize where it can best be used.

'*Thein to kuch karo Rajendra, kal favte gonti ler agyo*' ('Go and do something Rajendra, bring spade tomorrow and start work') said Mangu Lal Patel.

Notes

1   'Que Será, Será (Whatever Will Be, Will Be)' (1956) Words by Ray Evans, music by Jay Livingston, sung by Doris Day.

2   World3 was the computer model used to prepare *The Limits to Growth*. For the current status of this model, see D. Meadows, J. Randers and D. Meadows (2004) *Limits to Growth: The 30-Year Update*, Earthscan, London.

3   For example, J. Robinson (2003) 'Future subjunctive: Backcasting as social learning', *Futures*, vol 35, pp839–856.

4   See www.unep.org/geo/geo3

5   J. W. Forrester (1993) 'System dynamics and the lessons of 35 years', in K. B. De Greene (ed) *A Systems-Based Approach to Policymaking*, Kluwer, Boston, MA.

6   J. W. Forrester (1961) *Industrial Dynamics*, MIT Press, Cambridge, MA.

7   System dynamics modelling platforms with such
     graphical user interfaces include Dynamo, iThink,
     PowerSim, Stella, Vensim and Simile, our modelling
     environment of choice.

8   D. Meadows (1999) *Leverage Points: Places to Intervene
     in a System*, Sustainability Institute, Hartland, VT.

9   See opposite page for details of how to get this CD.

10   J. W. Forrester (1969) *Urban Dynamics*, Pegasus
     Communications, Waltham, MA.

11   N. Roberts (1978) 'Teaching dynamic feedback
     systems thinking: An elementary view', *Management
     Science*, vol 24, pp836–843. See also the Creative
     Learning Exchange at www.clexchange.org/, and J.
     Hight (1995) 'System dynamics for kids', *MIT News*,
     vol 98, no 2, http://sysdyn.clexchange.org/sdep/
     papers/D-4489-1.pdf

12   They are good. The current champion, the Hydra
     supercomputer, is estimated to have a FIDE rating
     over 3000, whereas the highest rating ever achieved
     by a human was 2851 by Gary Kasparov in 1999. See
     http://en.wikipedia.org/wiki/ELO_rating_system.

13   See http://en.wikipedia.org/wiki/Advanced_Chess.

14   Support for this contention is given by the defeat
     of the Hydra supercomputer by Vladimir Kramnik
     supported by a modest personal computer. Kramnik
     is currently the world champion in both classical and
     advanced chess. See http://en.wikipedia.org/wiki/
     Vladimir_Kramnik

15   Cited in David Reed (2004) *A Balanced Introduction
     to Computer Science*, Prentice Hall, Englewood Cliffs,
     NJ.

Resources

This section is not intended to be an exhaustive list of resources; instead it is a selected list that we have found useful. It includes works cited in the text, as well as others that may be useful although not directly quoted from in this book.

This list of resources is reproduced on this book's supporting website (and on the CD for those without web access), with links to the material. The website can be accessed at www.cifor.cgiar.org/RealizingFutures and the CD version is available free of charge from Realizing Community Futures CD-ROM, CIFOR, PO Box 6596 JKPWB, Jakarta 10065, Indonesia.

Preface

Lao Tzu (6th century BC) 'Care at the Beginning', Chapter 64a of *Tao Te Ching*, (translated by Peter A. Merel, 1995) available at www.chinapage.org/gnl.html

Vanclay, J. K., Prabhu, R. and Sinclair, F. (2003) 'Participatory modelling of community forest landscapes', *Small-scale Forest Economics, Management and Policy*, vol 2, pp117–326

Chapter 1 — Bringing shared visions to life

ACM (Adaptive Collaborative Management) website hosted by CIFOR at www.cifor.cgiar.org/acm

Colfer, C. J. P. (2005) *The Equitable Forest: Diversity and Community in Sustainable Resource Management*, Resources for the Future, Washington, DC

Hare, M., Letcher, R. and Jakeman, A. J. (2003) 'Participatory modelling in natural resource management: A comparison of four case studies', *Integrated Assessment*, vol 4, pp62–72

Mutimukuru, T., Nyirenda, R. and Matose, F. (2004) 'Learning amongst ourselves: Adaptive forest management through social learning in Zimbabwe', in Colfer, C. J. P. (ed) *The Equitable Forest: Diversity and Community in Sustainable Resource Management*, Resources for the Future, Washington, DC, pp186–206

Padre, S. (2000) 'Harvesting the monsoon: Livelihoods reborn. Centre for Information on Low External Input and Sustainable Agriculture', *ILEIA Newsletter*, March, pp14–15

Vernooy, R. and McDougall, C. (2003) 'Principles for good practice in participatory research: Reflecting on lessons from the field', in B. Pound, S. Snapp, C. McDougall and A. Braun (eds) *Managing Natural Resources for Sustainable Livelihoods: Uniting Science and Participation*, Earthscan/IDRC, London

Chapter 2 — Diverse interests and common problems

Brooke, T. H. (1808) *A History of the Island of St Helena from its Discovery by the Portuguese to the Year 1806*, Black, Parry & Kingsbury, London

Colfer, C. J. P. (1995) 'Who counts most in sustainable forest management?' Working Paper No 7, Center for International Forest Research, Bogor, Indonesia

Colfer, C. J. P. (2005) *The Complex Forest: Communities, Uncertainty, and Adaptive Collaborative Management*, Resources for the Future, Washington, DC

Darwin, C. (1859) *The Origin of Species*, John Murray, London

Diamond, J. (1995) 'Easter Island's end', *Discover Magazine*, vol 16, no 8, pp51–57

Diamond, J. (2005) *Collapse: How Societies Choose to Fail or Succeed*, Viking, New York

Hartanto, H., Lorenzo, M. C. and Frio, A. L. (2002) 'Collective action and learning in developing a local monitoring system', *International Forestry Review*, vol 4, pp184–195

Hartanto, H., Lorenzo, M. C., Valmores, C., Arda-Minas, L., Burton E. M. and Prabhu, R. (2003) *Learning Together: Responding to Change and Complexity to Improve Community Forests in the Philippines*, EarthPrint, Stevenage, UK

Hope, A. and Timmel, S. (1995) *Training for Transformation*, 3 vols, ITDG Publishing, Rugby, UK; Hope, A. and Timmel, S. (1999) *Training for Transformation, Book 4: A Handbook for Community Workers*, ITDG Publishing, Rugby, UK

Kamoto, J. and Milner, J. (2003) 'Negotiating multiple and overlapping claims on land rights: Experiences from Malawi', Hawaii International Conference on Social Sciences, Honolulu, Hawaii

Kant, S. and Berry, R. A. (2005) *Institutions, Sustainability and Natural Resources*, Springer, New York

Margulis, L. (1998) *Symbiotic Planet: A New Look at Evolution*, Basic Books, New York

Margulis, L. and Sagan, D. (2000) *What is Life?* University of California Press, Berkeley, CA

Martinez, M. (1999) 'An investigation into how successful learners learn: Measuring the impact of learning orientation, a learner-difference variable, on learning', Dissertation, Brigham Young University, University Microfilms No. 992217, Provo, UT

Mayers, J. (2005) *Stakeholder Power Analysis*, IIED, London

Mutimukuru, T., Kozanayi, W. and Nyirenda, R. (2006) 'Catalyzing collaborative monitoring processes in joint forest management situations: The Mafungautsi forest case, Zimbabwe', *Society and Natural Resources*, vol 19, pp209–224

Vania, F. and Taneja, B. (2005) *People, Policy, Participation: Making Watershed Management work in India*, IIED, London

Wenger, E. (1998) *Communities of Practice*, Cambridge University Press, Cambridge, www.ewenger.com/theory/index.htm

Chapter 3 — Shared visions

Borrini-Feyerabend, G., Pimbert, M., Farvar, M. T., Kothari, A. and Renard, Y. (2004) *Sharing Power: Learning by Doing in Co-management of Natural Resources throughout the World*, IIED, London, www.iied.org/sarl/pubs/otherpubs.html

Colfer, C. J. P., Prabhu, R., Günter, M., McDougall, C., Porro, N. M. and Porro, R. (1999) *Who Counts Most? Assessing Human Well-Being in Sustainable Forest Management*, C&I Tool No 8, CIFOR, Bogor, Indonesia

Costanza, R. (2000) 'Visions of alternative (unpredictable) futures and their use in policy analysis', *Ecology and Society* (formerly *Conservation Ecology*), vol 4, no 1, article 5, www.consecol.org/vol4/iss1/art5/

Hagmann, J. R., Chuma, E., Murwira, K., Connolly, M. and Ficarelli, P. (2002) 'Success factors in integrated natural resource management R&D: Lessons from practice', *Ecology and Society* (formerly *Conservation Ecology*), vol 5, no 2, article 29, www.ecologyandsociety.org/vol5/iss2/art29/

King. M. L. (1963) Address at Lincoln Memorial in Washington DC, 28 August, available at www.americanrhetoric.com/speeches/Ihaveadream.htm

Mapedza, E. (2005) 'Precaution in the designation and management of forest reserves in Zimbabwe: The case of Mafungautsi', in Cooney, R. and Dickson, B. (eds) *Biodiversity and the Precautionary Principle: Risk and Uncertainty in Conservation and Sustainable Use*, Earthscan, London

Meadows, D. (1994) 'Envisioning a sustainable world', Paper to 3rd Biennial Meeting of the International Society for Ecological Economics, 24–28 October, San José, Costa Rica

Moote, M. A., McClaran, M. P. and Chickering, D. K. (1997) 'Theory in practice: Applying participatory democracy theory to public land planning' *Environmental Management*, vol 21, pp877–889

Prabhu, R., Haggith, M., Mudavanhu, H., Muetzelfeldt, R., Standa-Gunda, W. and Vanclay, J. K. (2003) 'ZimFlores: A model to advise co-management of the Mafungautsi Forest in Zimbabwe', *Small-scale Forest Management, Economics and Policy*, vol 2, pp185–210

Ribot, J. C. (1997) *Ode to the Lorax*, Center for Population and Development Studies, Harvard University, Connecticut, www.ippnw.org/MGS/V5N2Lorax.html

Richardson, G. P. and Andersen, D. F. (1995) 'Teamwork in group model-building', *System Dynamics Review*, vol 11, pp113–137

Stack, J., Dorward, A., Gondo, T., Frost, P., Kurebgaseka, N. and Taylor, T. (2003) 'Mopane worm utilisation and rural livelihoods in Southern Africa', paper for Conference on Rural Livelihoods, Forest and Biodiversity, CIFOR/INWENT/BMZ/GTZ International, Bonn, Germany, May

Vanclay, J. K. (1998) 'FLORES: For exploring land use options in forested landscapes', *Agroforestry Forum*, vol 9, pp47–52

Vanclay, J. K. (2003) 'Why model landscapes at the level of households and fields?' *Small-scale Forest Management, Economics and Policy*, vol 2, pp121–134

Vanclay, J. K., Haggith, M. and Colfer, C. J. P. (2003) 'Participation and model-building: Lessons learned from the Bukittinggi workshop', *Small-scale Forest Management, Economics and Policy*, vol 2, pp135–154

Vennix, J. A. M. (1996) *Group Model-Building: Facilitating Team Learning Using System Dynamics*, John Wiley & Sons, Chichester (awarded the 1999 Forrester Award by the System Dynamics Society)

Chapter 4 — Explicit visions

The Bridge software package, available for download at www.cifor.cgiar.org/acm/pub/co-learn.html.

Hawkins, R. (undated) *Systems Diagrams Guidelines*, ICRA, Wageningen, The Netherlands

Leech, J. W., McMurtrie, R. E., West, P. W., Spencer, R. D. and Spencer, B. M. (1988) *Modelling Trees, Stands and Forests*, Bulletin No 5, School of Forestry, University of Melbourne, Melbourne

Lightfoot, C. (1987) 'Indigenous research and on-farm trials', *Agricultural Administration and Extension*, vol 24, pp79–89

Muetzelfeldt, R. and Massheder, J. (2003) 'The Simile visual modelling environment', *European Journal of Agronomy*, vol 18, pp345–358

Muetzelfeldt, R. and Taylor, J. (2002) 'Developing forest models in the Simile visual modelling environment', unpublished manuscript

Ross, D. (2005) Quoted in 'Sharon won't be fenced in' by Stewart Ain, *The Jewish Week*, 26 August, www.thejewishweek.com/news/newscontent.php3?artid=11303

Simile modelling and simulation software available for download, or for further information, at www.simulistics.com

Standa-Gunda, W., Mutimukuru, T., Nyirenda, R., Prabhu, R., Haggith, M. and Vanclay, J. K. (2003) 'Participatory modelling to enhance social learning, collective action and mobilization among users of the Mafungautsi Forest, Zimbabwe', *Small-scale Forest Management, Economics and Policy*, vol 2, pp313–326

Chapter 5 — Substantive visions

Goldsmith, Z. (1998) 'Back to the future in Rajasthan', *The Ecologist*, vol 28, July–August, p.222

Haggith, M. and Prabhu, R. (2003) 'Unlocking complexity: The importance of idealization in simulation modelling', *Small-scale Forest Economics, Management and Policy*, vol 2, pp293–312

Haggith, M., Muetzelfeldt, R. and Taylor, J. (2003) 'Modelling decision-making in rural communities at the forest margin', *Small-scale Forest Economics, Management and Policy*, vol 2, pp241–258

Kolb, D. A. (1986) *Experiential Learning: Experience as the Source of Learning and Development*, Prentice-Hall, Englewood Cliffs, NJ

Mahapatra, R. (1999) 'Waters of life', *Down to Earth*, 15 March, p38

Muetzelfeldt, R. and Massheder, J. (2003) 'The Simile visual modelling environment', *European Journal of Agronomy*, vol 18, pp345–358

Padre, S. (2000) 'Harvesting the monsoon: Livelihoods reborn', *ILEIA Newsletter*, March, p14–15

Shah, T. and Vengama Raju, K. (2000) 'Rethinking rehabilitation: Socio-ecology of tanks in Rajasthan, north-west India', International Water Management Institute, Colombo, Sri Lanka

Sharma, A. (2002) 'Does water harvesting help in water-scarce regions?', Paper to Annual Partners' Meet, IWMI-Tata Water Policy Research Program, International Water Management Institute, Colombo, Sri Lanka

Snedecor, G. W. and Cochran, W. G. (1980) *Statistical Methods*, 7th edition, Iowa University Press, Iowa City, IA

Srinivasan, R. K. and Babu, S. (2001) 'People fight back', *CatchWater*, vol 3, no 4, pp1–3

Tufte, E. (1983) *The Visual Display of Quantitative Information*, Graphics Press, Cheshire

Vanclay, J. K. (2003) 'The one-minute modeller: An introduction to Simile', *Annals of Tropical Research*, vol 25, pp31–44

Vanclay, J. K. and Skovsgaard, J. P. (1997) 'Evaluating forest growth models', *Ecological Modelling*, vol 98, pp1–12

Wenger, E. (1998) *Communities of Practices: Learning, Meaning and Identity*, Cambridge University Press, Cambridge

Ziman, J. (1978) *Reliable Knowledge: An Exploration of the Grounds for Belief in Science*, Cambridge University Press, Cambridge

Chapter 6 — Exploring alternatives

Ashby, J., Bergmark, C., Chandler, F. J. C., Dar, W. D., El-Beltagy, A., Erskine, W., Harrington, L., Harwood, R. R., Keatinge, D., Sanchez, P. A., Swift, M. and Walker, B. (2000) *Integrated Natural Resource Management Research in the CGIAR*, Penang, Malaysia, 25 August, www.inrm.cgiar.org/Workshop2000/Meeting%20Result/result.htm

Etienne, M., Le Page, C. and Cohen, M. (2003) 'A step-by-step approach to building land management scenarios based on multiple viewpoints on multi-agent system simulations', *Journal of Artificial Societies and Social Simulation*, vol 6, no 2, http://jasss.soc.surrey.ac.uk/6/2/2.html

Frost, R. (1915) 'The Road Not Taken', *Atlantic Monthly*, August. Currently available in most of the many editions of Frost's poems, such as the Library of America *Collected Poems, Prose, and Plays* (1995), and also widely reprinted in anthologies

Peterson, G. D., Cumming, G. S. and Carpenter, S. R. (2003) 'Scenario planning: A tool for conservation in an uncertain world', *Conservation Biology*, vol 17, pp358–366

Sebastian, S. (2003) 'Villagers' efforts washed away', *The Hindu*, 16 July

Sharma, A. (2002) 'Does water harvesting help in water-scarce regions?', paper to Annual Partners' Meet, IWMI-Tata Water Policy Research Program, International Water Management Institute, Colombo, Sri Lanka

Thapa, B., Walker, D. H. and Sinclair, F. L. (1997) 'Indigenous knowledge of the feeding value of tree fodder', *Animal Feed Science and Technology*, vol 67, pp97–114

Wollenberg, E., Edmunds, D. and Buck, L. (2000) *Anticipating Change: Scenarios as a Tool for Adaptive Forest Management: A guide*, CIFOR, Bogor, Indonesia

Chapter 7 — Into the Future

Forrester, J. W. (1961) *Industrial Dynamics*, MIT Press, Cambridge, MA

Forrester, J. W. (1969) *Urban Dynamics*, Pegasus Communications, Waltham, MA

Forrester, J. W. (1993) 'System dynamics and the lessons of 35 years', in K. B. De Greene (ed) *A Systems-Based Approach to Policymaking*, Kluwer, Boston, MA, available at http://sysdyn.clexchange. org/sdep/papers/D-4224-4.pdf

Hight, J. (1995) 'System dynamics for kids', *MIT News*, vol 98, no 2, available at http://sysdyn.clexchange.org/sdep/papers/D-4489-1.pdf

Meadows, D. (1999) *Leverage Points: Places to Intervene in a System*, Sustainability Institute, Hartland, VT

Meadows, D., Randers, J. and Meadows, D. (2004) *Limits to Growth: The 30-Year Update*, Earthscan, London

Roberts, N. (1978) 'Teaching dynamic feedback systems thinking: An elementary view', *Management Science*, vol 24, pp836–43

Robinson, J. (2003) 'Future subjunctive: Backcasting as social learning', *Futures*, vol 35, pp839–856

Index

acceptable performance 104
access 101
   rights to resources 14
action(s)
   collective 42
   identifying and planning 47
   learning 24
   of local people vs external
      experts 6
   research 42
   from scenarios to 139–40
   and visions 4, 35
actors 50, 54
adaptation 20, 27
adaptive collaborative management
   (ACM) 25, 27, 28, 42, 45, 98
address 100, 101
Africa 19, 27
age groups 15
agreement on common problem 7
agricultural extension agents 13
agriculture 42–3, 51
alternatives
   exploring 111–31
   and outcomes 114–22
Alwar district 115
apathy 22
appetite satisfaction 127
Asia 27

assumptions, substantiating 7
Atlantic Ocean 19
Ayurvedic medicine 33

backcasting 136
barter 97
Bataks 17
Batanai *see* broomgrass harvesters of
   Batanai
best guesses / 'best bet' strategy 93, 102,
   125–6
Bhikampura-Kishori village 73, 96
boundaries, delineation of 14
brainstorming sessions 101, 128
brewing beer 44
Bridge, The 71
BroomGrass case study/model 4–5, 6,
   15, 23, 36–40, 53, 81, 104, 106,
   126, 127
   Simile model 82, 83
      tidied up by experienced
        modeller 83
   simulations 117–18, 121
   whiteboard model 82–3
broomgrass harvesters of Batanai 3, 4–5,
   36–40, *37*, 38, 43, 52, 55, 105,
   106, 119, 124, 128, 139
brooms 37–40, 54, 55, 56, 121, 126
   beauty of 54, 127

tying 54, 56
Bush, George W. 67

calibration of model 93–7, 101–2, 107, 124, 137
cannibalism 19
Cape buffalo 43
capital, financial and social 42, 52
cash crops 97
caste 14
catchments 72, 116
chess 135, 136
   computer 139–40
children 15
   percentage in school 43
CIFOR (Centre for International Forest Research) 14, 130
   Adaptive Co-Management programme 117
civil war 19
class 14
clearing land 44
clouds 70
co-learner 24
Co-Learn package 50, 56
Colfer, Carol 14, 54
collaboration 18, 20, 22, 42
   learning and implications for management 26–8
collaborative management 43
collective action 42
common ground 65–8
common problems
   agreement on 7
   and diverse interests 9–28
communication
   barriers to 21
   of confidence 106–7
   and modelling 136
   networks 24
   team 102
   two-way 21
community/ies
   centres 14
   forest(s) 17, 23
      management 27
   of practice 23–4
compartments 69–70
competition 18, 130
complexity 16–18
computer 50
   based models 114, 135–6
   chess 139–40

generated simulations 47, 117
   see also simulations
Concepcion, island of Palawan 17
conceptualising 99
conduct, rules of 23
confabulation 102
confidence 56–7, 118
   building 104–7, 129–30
   communicating 106–7
conflict
   management 27
   resolution 136
conservation 43
construction poles 38
construction wood 44
cooperation 18
cotton 42, 43, 52
cropping 13, 44
crop(s) 6,
   cash 97
   growing 103
   residues 44
cultivating 44
culture, shared 23
current context 50, 51–2
cycles in models, rapid 99

dams 22, 45, 117
dark zone 71, 72, 94, 123
Dartmoor 56
Darwin, Charles 18
data collection 103
decision making 14, 20, 24, 27
   bodies, representation on 14
Deep Blue 139
Deep Thought 139
deforestation 19, 43
describing states 90–2
desired/desirable futures 50, 51
diagnosis of system 66
diagrams 69–71, 136
   development of 77
Diamond, Jared 19
Diana's Peak National Park 19
distribution of products 14
dreams
   'impossible' 129
   to visions from 31–45
drought 34

Easter Island 19
ecology 19

economics 18–19
ecosystems 12
education 56
  levels 15, 16
effective facilitation 24–6
Einstein, Albert 80, 106, 137, 140
elephants 43
employment
  alternative 43
  off-farm 44
empowerment 5
envisioning *see* visioning
ethnicity 14, 15
eucalyptus plantations, Ntonya Hill,
  Malawi 22–3
evaluation
  of model behaviour 102–4
  of scenarios 126–8
evaporation 72, 95
evolution 18, 20
experience, consolidating 130
experiential learning 19, 21
experiments
  analyse 67
  farmer-led 66–7

facilitation
  effective 24–6
  five-role system 48–9
facilitators 47, 48, 49
farmers 72
  experiments led by 66–7
  local 13
feedback loops 103, 130, 137
feral goats 19
fertilizing 44
field trips 130
fishing 19
  rights 100
five-role system of facilitation 48–9
flight simulators 131
floods 115
flows 69–70
focusing 98–9
food preparation 44
forecasting 114–15, 135
forest(s) 6, 13–14
  area 43
  collecting products 44
  community 17
  litter 44
  management 14, 15
  monitoring 17

patrols 56, 119, 120–1
resources 14, 52
sustainable managed 42
Forest Land Oriented Resource
  Envisioning System (FLORES)
  41–2
Forrester, Jay 136, 138
Freire, Paulo 22
Frost, Robert 111, 113
fruit 15, 43
  collecting 44
  selling 44
fuelwood 44
fund mobilization 14
future(s) 133–41
  desired/desirable 50, 51
  gearing up for 138

Gababe broomgrass collectors 118, 119,
  128
game 44
gardening 44
gatekeeper 48–9
gender 13, 15
Genesis mission 102
Global Environment Outlook 136
goats, feral 19
Gokwe district, Central Zimbabwe 39,
  42
Gopalpura, Rajasthan 90
granularity and scale 78–9
graphical user interfaces 136
graphs 99, 120
grass *see* broomgrass
grazing lands 52
grey models 71–6, 99
groundwater 5, 12
  extraction models of 69–75
  replenishment of 71
group discussions 130
Gwayi forest, Zimbabwe 41
Gweru Agricultural Show 3, 40

happiness 46
Hartanto, Herlina 17
harvesting 25, 26, 37, 44, 117
  illicit 41, 121
  sustainable 38, 120
health 46, 55
  care 56
  and nutrition 43
herding 44
honey 15, 38, 41, 43, 44

Hop, Anne 22
household
    decision-making 97
    maintenance 44
    wealth 97
hunting rights 100
hydroelectricity 13

idealization 97–100
identification of problem 66
implementing what has been learned 7
implications, exploring 7
incentives 43, 137
indicators and levers 50, 55–6
infiltration, typical 94
influences 70
Indonesia 42
industrial plantation 137
inflation 97
information deficits 12
infrastructure, maintaining 44
inorganic fertilizer 44
insects 43
intellectual property 105
intentional learning 27
interaction of people and natural
    resources 3
interests in resources 12–13
    diverse 14–15
intermediate variables 95–6
International Water Management
    Institute (IWMI) 94, 115–17,
    123, 128
inverted pyramid shape of johad in
    model 95, 96
irrigation 12, 13, 51, 123
Irrigation and Drainage Act 115
issue-oriented approach 124

johads (water percolation ponds) 35, 36,
    50, 52, 53, 72–6, 115, 128
    benefits 104
    calibration 93, 96
    design 76
    at Gopalpura, Rajasthan 90
    grey model 72
        multiple johads 75
        of river flow with varying
            numbers of johads 76
        with submodel structure 74
    inverted pyramid shaped 95, 96
    official opposition to 104

population 76
purpose 123
scale and granularity 78–9
simulations 115–17
slider to vary size during
    simulations 91–2
submodel 94–6
use of intermediate variables 95–6
joint enterprise 98

Kant, Shashi 18
Karanga-Shangwe people 43
Kariba, Lake 13, 43
Karnataka 117
Kasparov, Gary 139–40
King, Martin Luther 31, 33
knowledge
    representing 69–77
    shared 23
    synthesizing 20–1

labour 52
land
    cover 44
    tenure 100, 101
land-use
    decisions 6
    rights 100
    trends 13
Latin America 27
Lava Ka Baas dam 91, 117
leaders, village 13
leaf-branch-tree interactions, models of
    79
learning 19–20, 22
    collaboration and
    implications for management
        26–8
    from experience 19, 21
    intentional 27
    organizations 27
    through simulation 128–31
    structured 4, 6
leopards 43
levers and indicators 55–6
Lightfoot, Clive 66
lions 43
livelihood
    enhancement 14
    strategies 15
livestock 6, 15, 42, 43, 44, 52, 97, 103
Lorenzo, Chris 17

Mabhena, Mrs 38, 39
Madhya Pradesh 117
Mafa 37, 38
Mafungautsi region / State Forest,
    Zimbabwe
    resource sharing in 40–5
    see also ZimFlores case study/
        model
Mahapatra, Richard 96
maize 42, 43, 52, 97, 114
    stems 44
Malawi 22
management
    collaboration, learning and
        implications for 26–8, 43
    key issues 44
    systems 27
Mangu 52
manure 44, 103
maps 67–8, 81, 113
Margulis, Lynn 18
markets, new 38–9
Mars Climate Orbiter 102
Meadows, Donella 45, 137
Milner, James 22–3, 24
Miombo woodlands, Zimbabwe 42, 44
modeller 48
modelling
    aims and roles 98, 125, 136, 139
    benefits 113, 122, 125, 128
    computer 135, 138
    cycle 98, 124, 128, 130
    environments 92, 123
    participatory 4, 5, 6, 99, 117, 126,
        128, 129, 138, 141
    problem-based approach 124
    process 99, 104, 128
    system 70
    system dynamics 136, 138
    team 105
    techniques and skills 136, 138
    tree growth 79
    workshops 44, 48
models 69–84
    calibration 93–7, 101–2, 107
    communicating clearly 81–4
    completeness of 103
    confidence in 104–5
    describing states 90–2
    embellishments 72–3
    evaluating behaviour 102–4
    grey 71–6

humble beginnings 69–71
idealization 97–100
key resources and influences 80–1
knowing domain of utility 105–6
modelling cycle 98
quantifying relationships 92–102
re-examining assumptions 77–84
scale and granularity 78–9
simulation 5, 91
supporting structure 73–7
testing 107
understanding implications of 130–1
whiteboard 82–3
monitoring 25, 49, 55
monsoons 96, 116
mopane worm 43
mushrooms 43, 44
Mutimukuru, Tendayi 22

NASA 102
natural resources
    management 12, 17, 24, 27, 69, 98,
        140
    systems, interactions involved in 13
Ndebele 38, 43
negotiation 136
networking 18
Newton, Isaac 105–6, 137
non-timber forest products 15, 17, 139
Ntonya Hill, Malawi 22
nutrition and health 43
Nyirenda, Richard 4, 21, 24, 25, 37–40,
    83

Ocado, Francisco 66
ongoing learning 27
options, exploring 7
organizational issues 14
organizations, formal 24
outcomes, comparing 120–8
ownership
    examples of 100–1
    sense of 105

Pacific Ocean 19
Palawan 17
participation
    helping 66–7
    increased 38
participatory method 66–7
    analyse experiments 67
    define hypotheses 66–7

diagnose system 66
farmer-led experiments 66–7
identify problem 66
search for and screen
potential solutions 66
participatory modelling 4, 5, 6, 99, 117,
126, 128, 129, 138, 141
partnership 18
passiveness 21, 22
Patel, Mangu Lal 34–5, 51, 141
peer pressure 117, 118, 121, 124, 137
percolation tanks 6
Philippines 17
photographs 67–8, 81
photosynthesis 81
pictures
and symbols to map out vision 67–8
vs words 65
planning for future 113
plant growth, modelling 79, 80, 81
planting 44
ploughing 44
politicians 14
police 14
population
age profile 43
density 43
of johads 75
potential, recognition of 7
poverty 21, 44, 52
trap 42, 118
Power to Act, The 130
Power to Change, The 107
practice, communities of 23–4
problem-based approach 124
process coach 49
profit 39
prosperity 46
puzzle, hypothesize, test, reflect cycle
98–9, 128, 130

quality control 102
quantifying relationships 92–102

railway 55, 56
rainfall 6, 72, 78
calibration 94
Rajasthan 11, 33, 51, 68, 76, 117
Rajasthan Irrigation Department 117
Ramon Magsaysay award 11, 117
rangelands 6
rapid cycles in models 99
reasoning, experience-based 19

recognition of potential 7
recorder 48
reflection
learning, action cycle 117
puzzle, hypothesize, test and
reflect cycle 98, 128, 130
register 100, 101
relationships, quantifying 92–102
representing knowledge 69–77
resilience, building 18–28
resource(s)
allocation 25
conflicts 12
and influences 50, 52–47
management 39, 43, 45, 77, 97
committees (RMCs) 39, 43
sharing of 40–5
sustainable use 44, 119
-use problem 126
rhinoceros 43
Ribot, Jesse 41
rights 100–1
river flow 6, 115, 123
grey model of, with varying
numbers of johads 76
simulations 115–17
RiverMaker case study/model 5, 6,
11–28, 33–5, 50, 51, 52,
68– 79, 93–7, 102, 103–4, 106,
123, 124, 139
calibration 93–7, 124
simulations 115–17
road map 65–7
Roberts, Nancy 138
role-play 130
Ross, Dennis 65
route map 6–7
routines, shared repertoire of 23
rules
consistent 39
enforcement of 43
run button in Simile 89
Ruparel river 35, 91
rural development 43
agencies 13

safari hunting 43
St Helena 19
sale of products 14
San Rafael, island of Palawan 17
scale and granularity 78–9
scenario(s)
to actions 139–40

BroomGrass 38–9, 115–18
  evaluation 126–8
  exploration 16, 28, 46, 47, 48, 58,
    77, 102, 107
  extreme 129
  and modelling 113–14, 122, 124,
    129, 137
  RiverMaker 79, 116
  simulated 40, 50, 131, 136, 138
  for visioning 48, 114
  visions into 50
  ZimFlores 120–122
schools 43, 138
scribe 49
self-confidence 40
  gaining 104–5
self-development 25
self-esteem 46
selling
  produce 44
  vegetables 44
Shangwe 21, 43
shared learning 25
shared understanding 20–3, 24
shared visions 1–7, 31–57
sheep 19
Shona 21, 43
Sibanda, Liswe 54, 106–7
sickles 52
Simile model 71, 91–2, 99, 100, 101
  by broomgrass collectors 82, 83
  RiverMaker 94
  run button 89
simplifying 98
simulation models 5, 91, 114, 115–118,
    120, 128
  learning through 128–31
  understanding implications of 130–1
Singh, Rajendra 5, 11–12, 13, 15, 21,
    22, 24, 26, 33–5, 51, 52, 54, 55,
    68, 69, 71, 72, 73, 78, 91, 93,
    96, 115, 123, 139, 141
Siwela, Mrs 3, 36, 40
Siwela, Ramushe 36
slider to vary johads' size during
    simulations 91–2
social capital 6
social learning 42, 117, 118
  processes 27
social networks 42
social relations 44
soil, water retention capacity of 73
solution, focus on 124–5

stakeholders 13–14, 54, 81, 115, 122,
    125, 126, 127, 130
  relationships between 14
Standa-Gunda, Wavell 83
stover 44
strategies 50, 52
strategy games 99
structured learning 4, 5, 6
submodel 73–5, 97–8, 101, 102
  johad 74, 94–5
  surface water 93–4
substantiating assumptions 7
success, recognizing 122–8
surface water
  submodel 93–4
  typical 94
sustainable harvesting 38
sustainable managed forests 42, 119
sustainable resource use 44
survival of fittest 18, 20
symbols to map out vision 67–8
system dynamics 136–7
  packages 71

Tagbanuas 17
Tanabag, island of Palawan 17
Tarun Bhagat Sangh (TBS, Young India
    Association) 13, 115, 117
Tendayi 38
termitarium soil 44
testing model 98, 107, 128, 130
Thanagazi 33, 35, 51, 94
thatchgrass 15, 25, 38, 43, 139
timber
  illegal harvesting of 15
  –wildlife conflict 43
Timmel, Sally 22
title office 100
Tolawas Mala 96
Tonga 43
tourism 43
traders 14
transformation, training for 22, 25
transformative learning processes 27
transport 52
transporters 14
tree(s)
  architecture, models of 79
  cutting 44
trial and error approach 101
triangulation 97
typical infiltration 94
typical surface 94

uncertainty, dealing with 18–28
understanding, shared 20–3, 24
utility, knowing domain of 105–6

value, adding 117, 118, 126
variable parameter (in Simile) 91
variables 70, 101, 123
vegetable(s)
    gardens 52
    growing 42, 103
    selling 44
village
    leaders 13
    population 73
    water use 70, 71
visioning 21, 25, 28, 39, 46
    process 46–50
vision(s)
    to action 35
    building blocks of 50–6
        actors 50, 54
        current context 50, 51–2
        desired/desirable futures 50, 51
        indicators and levers 50, 55–6
        key resources and influences 50,
            52–4
        strategies 50, 52
    creating 45–56
    developing 50
    from dreams to 31–45
    explicit 7, 63–84
    -oriented approach 124
    shared 1–7, 31–57
    to substance 56–7
    substantive
visualization techniques 68
vlei 5, 6, 50, 52, 53

water 5, 6
    collecting 44
    engineers 13
    extraction models 69–71
    flow 115
    harvesting 12, 26, 34, 51, 77, 117
    improvement 51, 55, 69
    as key resource 52
    percolation ponds *see* johads
    retention 73
    scarcity 11–12, 34–5, 51
    stakeholders in 13
    surface 5

    use 70, 71, 73
    from wells 6, 55, 70, 71, 123
    see also groundwater
watering 44
wealth 13
weather
    forecasts 114–15, 135
    reports 113
web 16
weeding 44
Wenger, Etienne 23
whiteboard model 82–3, 99
wildlife–timber conflict 43
women 15, 21
    constructing johad *36*
    reluctance to engage in public
        discussions 22
workshops 24, 39–40, 43, 44, 48–50,
    99, 101
World Heritage Area 43
World3 135

Zambezi Valley 42
Zimbabwe 4, 21, 22, 36, 42, 119
Zimbabwe Forest Patrol Unit 53
Zimbabwe Forest Protection Unit 53
Zimbabwe Forestry Commission 15, 21,
    37, 41, 53
ZimFlores case study/model
    (Mafungautsi forest) 6, 13, 15,
    21, 22, 15, 36, 39, 52, 53, 56,
    100, 106, 114, 126, 139
    calibration, formulation and
        idealization 97–102
    simulations 119–22
Zomba, Malawi 22–3